author's life, from her teenage years to her marriage and motherhood. Like most of us, she ran into hard times with various people and struggled with thoughts of "Where am I missing it?" "How come God?" and "What am I doing wrong?" If each of us were honest, we would likely say we have been there or we are there now.

What caught my eye or got my attention as I began reading this book was Jeni's written account of her encounter with the Trinity—Father, Son, and Holy Spirit. She kept a written record of her encounters with God through prayer, keeping it simple and easy to follow, allowing her to document her thoughts, prayers, and what the Holy Spirit revealed to her or gave her a clearer understanding of. She also poses questions for the reader to ponder while reading her book. At the age of 86, when I look back, I can remember many hard or dry times in my walk with God. When reading this book, I noticed how repetitive Jeni's methods were in getting answers from her Father in Heaven. She stayed steady in her prayer time, kept her questions simple, remained in love with Jesus, and never blamed Him; she also learned to be patient with God and herself. We don't usually "get into trouble" overnight, so don't expect to overcome everything overnight!

This book is easy to follow, and as you read it, listen for the Holy Spirit as he speaks wisdom or understanding to you! This happened to me, and I wasn't even thinking of that when I first started to read the book! If the Holy Spirit spoke to me while reading this book, I believe He will do the same for others who read it.

—Jim Tyler
Redeeming Love Ministries

The same question Jesus asked His followers, He is asking you today: "Who do you say that I am?" In Scripture, the name of Jesus is woven with promises, power, and purpose. Time and again, we see that His name is more than just a word—it is a conduit for miracles, healing, and transformation. As we read in John 14:13, God promises, "I will do whatever you ask in my name."

Jeni LaGore invites us to embark on a journey of discovery that seeks to answer these questions and more. In *Who is Jesus to You?* Jeni leads us on an exploration of the profound significance of Jesus' name, encouraging us not only to utter it but also to understand the authority and grace behind it. This book is an invitation to reflect on the unique power of Jesus, a name that is above all others, and how that name can transform our lives. To know Jesus must be our glorious quest—this book will show you how! May this book draw you closer to Jesus, the One whose name is truly worthy of all honor, praise, and trust.

—Brian Simmons
Passion & Fire Ministries

The book you are holding is a beautiful labor of love! Jeni has brought the majesty, intricacy, and simplicity of Jesus to us all in this thoughtful work. We are thankful for the depth, scholarship, and delicate balance that her writing conveys. The carefully chosen words are a gift to those who need a fresh introduction to the Name from which all names derive. Best of all, Jeni knows, personally and intimately, the One she has written about—Jesus is truly Jeni's first and greatest love!

—Dan and Kayla Crist
Founding Pastors of 1Mosaic Church

It is our honor to offer a whole-hearted endorsement for Jeni LaGore's insightful book, *Who Is Jesus to You? Embracing the Reality of Knowing His Name.*

Jeni LaGore offers a profound yet practical guide to understanding the most beautiful, holy, and powerful name of all—the name above all names, Jesus. For those who have called upon His name, we are in awe of the reality that it is as multifaceted as His nature. This book is a refreshing invitation to move beyond abstract theology and truly engage with Jesus on a personal and transformative level—as Jeni puts it, "to embrace and take hold of His name."

What sets this book apart is its emphasis on the "practicality" of knowing Jesus. She challenges us to consider what that knowledge means for our daily decisions, relationships, and spiritual journey. Jeni is on a journey to know her Lord in ever-deepening awe and intimacy, and you will no doubt catch fire as you experience her passion expressed in every page. *Who Is Jesus to You?* will undoubtedly challenge, encourage, and inspire you. This book is both a precious gift and a powerful resource, lighting the way to a more intimate and impactful relationship with Jesus. Highly recommended!

—Jeremiah and Teresa Yancy
Authors, The Messenger Life
Founders, Unlocking Your Book

When the opportunity crossed my path to read Jeni LaGore's book, I gladly offered to do so. I have known her and her husband for about 20 years and have observed them before their marriage and right up until the present. Their personal lives have been tested time and time again, yet they stand strong and together in this world as an example for all to see!

I highly recommend *Who Is Jesus to You?* for several reasons. It is simple to read and understand. The book is a written account of the

Who is Jesus to You?

Who is Jesus to You?

EMBRACING THE REALITY OF KNOWING HIS NAME

Jeni LaGore

Messenger Books
30 N. Gould Ste. R
Sheridan, WY 82801

Contents

For Jesus, the Lover of my soul.

*For my husband, my stabilizer, thank you for loving
and believing in me throughout the years. Your constant support
made it possible for this dream to come true. And for my children,
my greatest desire is for you to continue in your wonderful pursuit
of knowing Jesus more intimately and practically every day.
Each of you has witnessed my wrestle as this message was forged
within me, and in a sense, have experienced the forging as well.
Every one of you is a testimony of God's mercy and grace in my life,
and I love you all more than words could ever express.*

*For those who want to explore and experience
every aspect of who Jesus is.*

Foreword

In the first chapter of the Gospel according to St. Luke, we encounter the angel Gabriel, who carries a message from Heaven to a young woman named Mary concerning a son whom she would bear.

This child, conceived by the Holy Spirit, would be the Son of God, Messiah, the long-awaited Promised One. Gabriel instructed Mary to name the child Yeshua, meaning "God Saves," for the salvation of humanity was His foreordained purpose.

In many cultures around the world, naming is a sacred rite that is integral in establishing how a person is perceived, socially accepted, and remembered for generations to come. One's name is thought to carry the power of identity.

Jeni LaGore has authored a book that takes the reader on a journey into the depths of "What's in a Name?" With surgical precision, she dissects the meaning of Jesus/Yeshua, God Saves, and several other titles by which He is called and made known.

 To know Jesus is the shortest description of true grace; to know Him better is the surest mark of growth in grace; to know Him perfectly is eternal life.

— John Newton

Each chapter of this book peels back another layer of revelation, allowing the reader to come to know Him perfectly, as the yielded soul is carried deeper, closer, unveiling and exposing aspects of the Lord's character that are often unexplored. As you travel with the author, there will be opportunities to pause and ponder what you have discovered, followed by the comforting, sometimes challenging, yet warm, embrace of prayer.

Should you endeavor to allow Jeni to lead you on this path (and I highly recommend that you do), a focused pursuit of knowing His Grace and Presence is your assignment; a revelation concerning "who Jesus is to you" will strengthen your faith, and a profound intimacy *with* Him and *in* Him is His special gift that awaits you.

And now fellow pilgrim, grab your Bible, settle down in a quiet comfortable place, breathe deeply, welcome Holy Spirit, and know that "I am asking God, the glorious Father of our Lord Jesus Christ, to give you spiritual wisdom and insight so that you might grow in your knowledge of God" (Ephesians 1:17 NLT).

Blessings Beloved, and Bon Voyage...

—Bernardine Wormley Daniels
Soterios Ministries, Inc.

Part One

Encounter

The Starting Point

Chapter 1

What Is in a Name?

When we pray "in the Name of Jesus,"
the answers are in accordance with His nature,
and if we think our prayers are unanswered, it is because we
are not interpreting the answer along this line.
—Oswald Chambers, *God's Workmanship*—

Ask me anything in my name, and I will do it for you!
—John 14:14—

Character in a saint means the disposition
of Jesus Christ persistently manifested.
—Oswald Chambers, *Devotional Reader*—

WHAT IS SO IMPORTANT ABOUT A NAME? ISN'T A NAME SIMPLY A source of identification, letters spelled out to identify people, places, and things? Maybe. But what about Jesus' name? There must be something different about His name.

Who Is Jesus to You?

Scripture attaches power and promise to the name of Jesus. Several times in the Gospel of John, Jesus instructed His followers to believe and ask in His name, indicating that His name has the power to invoke a response. For example, John 14:13 states, "I will do whatever you ask me to do when you ask me in my name." Does this really mean that by simply saying the name of Jesus, we get whatever we ask?

What is so unique about "Jesus" that He wants us to believe in and ask in His name? How do we ask "in" a name? Do we do so by simply tacking on "in Jesus' name" to the end of our prayers? There must be more.

The following pages contain an in-depth study of what makes Jesus' name so exceptional. Let's go on a wondrous journey of discovery and set a course for exploring the One who has the name above all.

At the Altar

Several years ago, in a small church where I frequently encountered God, I stood at the altar. Typically, I would step out from my usual seat in the second row and approach the altar during worship. In that space, distractions melted away, and I became swept up in the presence of Jesus. I felt increased freedom to sing with everything in me. It was my hope that the music would drown the sound of my voice. (No one has ever confirmed or corrected this theory of mine; I wish to keep it that way.)

This particular weekday evening, we sang "Break Every Chain" by Will Reagan about the power of Jesus' name. Many songs lead our hearts to the Lord's heart, reaching deep within and drawing us closer to Him and His purpose, but that song just does something in me. It always has.

That night, after singing along for a short while, I began to pour my heart out to Jesus. I said something like, "Lord, I believe there is power in Your name. I believe Your Word and that You are who the Scriptures declare You are. You have proven Yourself to me time and time again. I believe there is power in Your name to break every chain of bondage. So, why are things and situations in my life not bowing to Your name—things I have prayed about again and again? I have taken authority in Your name, just like You instructed, but these troubles are not bowing or breaking. What am I missing?"

I try to be real with myself and honest before God. I have learned it does me no good to overlook my shortcomings. I want to be more like Jesus every day, and I believe that requires self-examination. So I ask the hard questions. I ask humbling and sometimes painful questions about myself because I know transformation and freedom come through embracing hard but life-changing truths.

In addition to being introspective, I am also very practical. If we cannot apply Jesus to our everyday situations, then we only have head knowledge. Head knowledge without action accomplishes little to nothing. I equate it to religion without relationship, "having a form of godliness but denying its power" (2 Timothy 3:5 NIV).

So, there I was, standing at the altar, silently asking Jesus about specific situations where I had proclaimed His name and not seen change. I was being raw and honest. I needed Him to work in some areas, and I was quite desperate to understand so that I could get different results—*divine results.*

In the quiet of my heart, I heard the Lord say, "Look up the meaning of 'name.'" I was stunned.

Never in all my years of being a follower of Jesus and studying the Bible had I ever thought to look into what "name" meant. It hadn't seemed to be a word with a definition beyond my understanding. Apparently, it was. My curiosity was piqued.

Meaning and Purpose

God is particular about names. He named Adam according to what He formed him from. Adam means "son of the red earth" in Hebrew. He renamed Abram and Sarai and assigned the name Isaac to their promised son. Each name had meaning and purpose. God was especially intentional when naming His Son. Although we know Him as Jesus Christ, in Hebrew, His name is *Yeshua HaMashiach. Yeshua* means "salvation," and *HaMashiach* means "the Anointed One."[1]

Scripture points to Jesus as the one anointed to be our source of salvation. Father God named His Son with meaning and purpose.

Peter testified to the truth of Jesus as our source of salvation in Acts 4:12: "There is no one else who has the power to save us, for there is only one name to whom God has given authority by which we must experience salvation: *the name of Jesus.*" Interestingly, Peter connected the name of Jesus to salvation and authority.

The apostle John spoke of authority in correlation to Jesus' name as well. In John 1:12, he said, "Those who embraced him and took hold of his name were given authority to become the children of God!" In most translations, this verse reads, "Those who received Him and believed in His name." Receiving and believing basically mean accepting and acknowledging. However, to "embrace and take hold of" is much richer, indicating intimacy, intention, and action. If embracing and taking hold of Jesus' name gives us the authority to become children of God, then exploring a deeper meaning of the word "name" is worth our time.

Name: What Does It Really Mean?

The day after my interaction with the Lord at the altar, I did as He told me. I discovered that "name" is the Greek word *onoma*, and it means "authority" or "character." It comes from a presumed derivative that means "to know absolutely."

Practically, we could exchange "name" with "authority" in John 1:12, and doing so opens a deeper understanding: "Those who embrace him and take hold of his [authority] are given authority to become children of God." Taking hold of the authority that is in Him gives us the authority to become His children.

Let's do the same with the word "character": "Those who embrace him and take hold of his [character] are given authority to become children of God." To take hold of His character implies we take it unto ourselves. We live it out, shape our lives by it, and mirror our character after the character of Jesus. We must seek to understand and know the character of Jesus in order to take hold of it.

To Know...Absolutely

Let's take a look at the definition of the words "know" and "absolutely." The basic meaning of both is typically understood; however, a closer look brings deeper revelation.

- **Know** —"to perceive directly: have direct cognition of; to recognize the nature of; to be acquainted or familiar with; to have experience of; to be aware of the truth or factuality of; be convinced or certain of; to have a practical understanding of"[2]
- **Absolutely** — "completely or totally"[3]

To know Jesus is to perceive Him directly, which brings personal cognition or awareness of Him through our minds and senses. He longs to be known by us according to His nature, not our preconceived ideas based on our human relationships or experiences.

As we seek to be acquainted with Him, He provides us with personal experiences with Him that are always in alignment with the truths in Scripture. Through our experiences with Him, we become convinced and certain of His truth and the factuality of who He is.

It truly delights His heart when we purpose to have a practical understanding of Him through His Word and our personal relationship with Him. This is the action of "embracing Him and taking hold of His name."

Absolutely, completely, totally... This is how Jesus wants us to know Him. There is no restriction in developing our relationship with Him, except that which we ourselves create. There is no limitation on the time we spend with Him, for upon invitation, He comes and makes His home in us. Thus, our comprehension of Jesus' authority and character begins and continues when we seek to know Him, absolutely.

More Insight Into "Name"

Further study of the meaning of "name" supplies even greater insight. As I read the following definitions[4] for the first time, my spirit was swirling, overwhelmed by the deepening of my understanding of the power of the name above every other name—Jesus.

A Name Is the Manifestation
or Revelation of Someone's Character

A "manifestation" is "a perceptible, outward, or visible expression."[5] "Revelation" is an act of revealing something or someone to be viewed or known by others. It is also "an act of revealing or communicating divine truth."[6]

Thinking of the words in John 1:12, "Those who embraced and took hold of his name," manifestation and revelation aren't words to be ignorant of. When we embrace and take hold of Jesus' name, we take possession of it and thus manifest His character, revealing Him and His ways to the people around us. We make Him clear and obvious, openly seen and known, through our words, behaviors, and actions.

A Name Distinguishes a Person from All Others

To "distinguish" is "to perceive a difference in" or "to mark as separate or different." The origin of this word literally means "to separate by pricking."[7] This is an interesting fact to note because it is in the pricking circumstances of life that one's true character is revealed. For example, when a patient person is inconvenienced by disrupted plans, they remain calm and seek a solution. Whereas, an impatient person may lose their temper and allow frustration to dominate their emotions.

Jesus' character definitely set Him apart. The people perceived a difference in Him compared to the religious leaders of His day, who pricked Him repeatedly with tests, challenges, and questions regarding His authority. By taking hold of Jesus' character, we, too, become marked as separate or different—*distinguished.*

To Pray in Jesus' Name Is to Pray as Directed and Authorized by Him

To pray as directed or authorized by Him, we must listen for His voice before we use ours. He alone knows each person's heart, and He knows the end from the beginning. He will direct our prayers accordingly.

Praying in Jesus' name has a prerequisite: being in His presence, not merely for a period of time each day, but at all times. The two most commonly used words for "presence" in Hebrew are "before" and "face." We must live before the face of God. When we look into His face, we are able to hear Him direct our lives and words.

Bringing Revelation That Flows Out
of Being in His Presence

To pray in Jesus' name is to bring revelation that flows out of being in His presence. Thus, we can pray in His name without saying "Jesus." He communicates divine truth to us as we humbly listen. When we ask anything in Jesus' name, we simply ask according to what Jesus directed us to ask for; hence, Father God responds.

When we speak by way of revelation that flows from being in His presence, we release on earth what has already been released in Heaven.

A Name Is Inseparable from the Person
to Whom It Belongs—It Is His Essence

Take a moment to digest that. When we say the name of Jesus, we are speaking Him, His person.

The essence of a person is their individual nature. It is their "most significant element, quality, or aspect."[8] To speak the name of Jesus is to release who He is and all that He embodies.

The Word of God unveils Jesus' nature and His most significant elements and qualities. Reading the Gospels reveals His depth of love and compassion, His heart of justice and obedience to His Father, and His perseverance and commitment.

Since Jesus and Holy Spirit are one, His nature is defined in Galatians 5:22–23 as the fruit of the Spirit: love, joy, peace, patience, goodness, kindness, gentleness, faithfulness, and self-control. Absolutely everything about Jesus is held in His name. To embrace and take on His name is to embrace and take on His essence.

Practically Speaking

Let's think of it this way. When business owners hire someone, the employee represents the company and its products and services. They aren't employed to promote their own agenda. The employee is empowered by the company to promote the cause and reputation of the company. To be most effective, the employee must have full knowledge and understanding of all the company's products and services, policies, and procedures. The more they fully embrace the mission and goal of their employer, the more effective they are in their work. The more time they spend with the owner, the more efficiently they can communicate the mission, goal, and overall heart and purpose of the company. Over time, the employee is able to represent the company as if it were their own.

So it is with us in our individual relationships with Jesus. When we embrace and take hold of the name of Jesus, we are taking Him, His essence, within ourselves. This action is life-altering. The character and nature of each believer begin to morph into the likeness of His character and nature. We become so connected with the person of Jesus that the words coming out of our mouths are actually coming out of His.

In relation to my story, Jesus heard me at the altar that night and graciously answered me. In His wisdom, He didn't simply answer my question by creating a checklist of what I needed to do in order to see situations change. While He wants to lead us to victory in our areas of challenge, He isn't a taskmaster. His nature is to lovingly support and lead us into victory through intimate relationship with Him. By leading me into a search to discover what "name" means, He did exactly that.

As I learned the truths He revealed, it became clear why situations were not changing. I was expecting His power to manifest and bring the solution to my need simply because the name Jesus was rolling off my tongue.

In some areas of my life, His character was not being manifested or revealed; therefore, I lacked His authority. At first, I was confused because I regularly spent time reading the Bible and praying. My mind was on Jesus often. But I came to understand that there were still areas in my heart that needed to *know* His name.

Learning His Name

A name is a declaration of who a person is. In order to fully know who Jesus is to you, it is imperative to know His name—or rather, His names, for He has many. Each of His names defines a portion of His character and nature. His *essence*.

The simple search I began in order to understand my lack when proclaiming the name of Jesus has led me to a deeper, ever-growing search of who He is. The more I search, the more I learn. The more I learn, the more I know Him. The more I know Him, the more I love Him and desire to embrace and take hold of His name.

The process of knowing who Jesus is isn't meant to be quick. It is not a race but rather a life journey. He walks with us as we seek. Be assured that as you seek Him with all your heart, you will find Him. He loves to reveal Himself to those longing to know Him.

In the chapters to follow, I present several names of Jesus that are simple and practical. Some are traditional and well-known, some are untraditional and largely unknown. However, each one is found or implied within the written Word of God and describes the authority, character, nature, and essence of who Jesus is. My hope is that by exploring these practical names of Jesus, together we will begin to experience the fullness of His name—embracing the practicality of *knowing* Him.

Maybe you are like me—a believer who has spoken the name of Jesus countless times yet is not fully aware of what His name represents or the power it holds. Maybe you are just beginning your exploration of who Jesus is. (If so, congratulations!) Wherever you are in your spiritual walk, I am thrilled to be a part of your journey. No matter who you are, your background, or the length of time you have been seeking Jesus, He is madly in love with you. He knows your name. He desires you to know His. Absolutely.

Points to Ponder

- List one element of the definition of "name" that spoke to your heart, and spend some time meditating on it.
- How does this shift your understanding of the name of Jesus?

Prayer of Embrace

Lord Jesus, I long to know You, absolutely. Reveal to me the essence of who You are as I read Your Word and seek Your face. Help me develop Your character as my own. Teach me to walk in Your ways. As I spend time in Your presence, manifest Yourself and deposit revelation within me. As I sit at Your feet, may I absorb Your essence and become distinguished as one who embraces and has taken hold of Your name. Amen.

Chapter 2

Who Do You Say I Am?

There is a world of difference between knowing the
Word of God and knowing the God of the Word.
—Leonard Ravenhill, *Why Revival Tarries—*

Sheer scholarship alone cannot reveal to us the gospel
of grace. We must never allow the authority of books,
institutions, or leaders to replace the authority of
KNOWING Jesus Christ personally and directly.
—Brennan Manning, *The Ragamuffin Gospel—*

We should remember that people can go to Heaven without
knowing much of the Word of God, but they cannot go to
Heaven without knowing Jesus Christ as Savior.
—Lee Roberson—

Believe it or not, it is possible to follow Jesus and not
fully know who He is. In the days that He walked the earth, masses
of people sought Jesus for help because of the stories they had heard
—stories of those who had encountered His touch and received heal-

ings, deliverance, and miracles. Yet, even amongst those who had received from Him or witnessed the signs and wonders firsthand were many who still questioned who this man, Jesus, was.

In our world today, who He truly is doesn't seem to be widely known. Yet He desires that all would know Him intimately and practically. We must search within ourselves to discover how well we know Jesus. With an open heart, we can honestly assess who He is to us and why. Jesus once posed an interesting question to His disciples: Who do you say that I am? He pressed them to settle this question within their spirit, and we can assume that He asks us to do the same.

Believing Personally

As a young girl who attended church semi-regularly, I assumed I was a Christian because I believed in God. I had heard about Father, Son, and Holy Spirit and believed in them as the Triune Godhead. While my heart was drawn to Jesus, I lacked the understanding that I could know Him personally and intimately.

As a young adult, I transitioned from knowing *about* Jesus to *knowing* Him personally by opening the door of my heart for Him to come live in me. Later, when my husband and I had children, we taught them according to our faith. While they were still quite young, I often explained that they would need to decide to believe in and know Jesus for themselves.

One day during our Bible time, my firstborn daughter courageously said, "Mom, I know I believe because this is what you and Dad have taught us, but I'm not sure I believe it for myself." Tears welled up in my eyes—not out of sadness, but joy.

My child was thinking for herself, processing information, and truly contemplating her own beliefs. She had acquired enough information to know *about* Jesus, but this day marked the beginning of her journey to *know* Him, to explore and discover who Jesus was for herself. This is the journey all must take.

Three questions

After Jesus' disciples had been following Him for quite some time, He asked them three questions regarding His true identity. We find the dialogue in Matthew 16:13–16:

> When Jesus came to Caesarea Philippi, he asked his disciples this question: "What are the people saying about me, the Son of Man? Who do they believe I am?" They answered, "Some are convinced you are John the Baptizer; others say you are Elijah reincarnated, or Jeremiah, or one of the prophets." "But you—who do you say that I am?" Jesus asked. Simon Peter spoke up and said, "You are the Anointed One, the Son of the living God!"

I moved past Jesus' first two questions without any thought for years, focusing more on the answer to His third question. Now, however, I can't help but ponder the intent of His first two questions. "What are the people saying about me, the Son of Man? Who do they believe I am?" He probably already knew the answer, for He knows the thoughts of men.[1]

Jesus may have asked these questions to provoke the disciples to explore their own hearts as to who He was and discover for themselves if they aligned with the opinions of the crowd, or if their personal experience with Him brought a different revelation. After hearing their response, Jesus then asked, "But who do you say that I am?"

He went from asking what the word on the street was about Him to asking what they thought for themselves. Peter quickly responded,

"You are the Christ, Son of the Living God." By acknowledging Jesus as the Christ, he declared Him the Anointed One, the long-awaited Messiah. He had been with Jesus long enough to witness the reality of what Jesus proclaimed in the synagogue when He said, "The Spirit of the Lord is upon me, and he has anointed me to be hope for the poor, healing for the brokenhearted, and new eyes for the blind, and to preach to prisoners, 'You are set free!' I have come to share the message of Jubilee, for the time of God's great acceptance has begun" (Luke 4:18–19).

Peter had connected Jesus' bold proclamation to His actions. His spiritual eyes were opened; he *knew* Him.

The disciples walked with Jesus, day after day. They were closest to Him, heard each of His messages, and were attentive when Jesus privately explained hidden meanings within His parables. They had seen His response to requests, criticisms, questions, tests, and temptations. The disciples knew Jesus personally and more intimately than the masses who followed Him.

The questions Jesus posed are just as much for us now as they were for His disciples then. With these questions, the distinction is made between those who followed Him from time to time versus those who walked with Him daily. They identified those with head knowledge versus those with heart knowledge—intimate connection versus distant interaction. Jesus' questions drew the line between knowing *about* Him and truly *knowing* Him.

Knowledge vs. Knowing

As we learned in the previous chapter, *knowing* is more than having cognitive knowledge. *Knowing* Jesus, therefore, goes beyond knowing facts about Him, believing in Him, or receiving a blessing from Him. *Knowing* Him includes having an experience that creates a certainty of who He is in a practical way.

Who Is Jesus to You?

In today's world, with the internet and social media providing information at our fingertips, we can know things about people that we have never met. Yet even with that information, they are strangers to us.

Knowing someone's name and a few facts about them because you cross paths makes them an acquaintance. This type of relationship is surface-level, but nothing too personal.

Knowledge does not equal *knowing*, and interaction does not equal an intimate connection. It is only in pursuing others that we begin to *know* them. Over time, we become familiar with someone's character and nature and gain a practical understanding of who they are. But if we do not pursue growth in that relationship, it remains superficial.

The same is true of our knowledge of Jesus. Knowing about Him, even if we have known about Him our entire lives, doesn't equal *knowing* Him. Going to church and reading our Bible, while very good, do not indicate being intimately connected to Christ. We must *embrace and take hold of His name*, entering into union with Him. Our spirit must be mingled with His.[2]

The importance of knowing God by experience caused me to pray for my children before having them. Regularly, I declared that they would not just know about God (head knowledge) but *know* Him (heart knowledge). In my imperfection, I did my best to teach them how to pursue a personal relationship with Jesus.

As we seek to *know* Jesus, we grow in our relationship with Him. As we grow in our understanding of His nature and His ways, we experience His goodness more and more. We can walk through times of peace as well as trials, confident that He is with us. With each experience, we *know* Him with more certainty in the depths of our hearts.

While He desires to have ever-increasing interaction and intimacy with us, He has granted us free will. It is possible to keep Jesus as an acquaintance and miss out on a personal connection with Him. He allows us the space to determine the pace and depth to which we know Him.

We must be willing to evaluate our relationship with Jesus. Do we have head knowledge but lack intimacy with Him? Have we limited our faith in Jesus by the beliefs and opinions of others? Are we content with receiving from His goodness as needed, or are we faithfully in pursuit of *knowing* Him more?

Regardless of where we are in our relationship with Jesus, He is open for dialogue. He initiated the conversation with His disciples, and He awaits conversation with each of us as well. We, too, must identify what we have heard and explore how it has affected us. Jesus is good at helping us sort it all out, and I believe He enjoys the process.

Knowing His Name in the Old Testament

Throughout the Old Testament, many names were ascribed to God, according to His characteristics and how He made Himself known. These names also belong to Jesus, since Jesus is God.[3]

Beginning in Genesis 1, God is commonly known as *Elohim,* which could be translated as "Mighty God," stressing His sovereignty and power.[4] God is referred to as *Yahweh-Elohim* in Genesis 2, which means "the God who is Yahweh" or "the God of mercy and power."[5] In Genesis 14, we learn the name *El Elyon,* which means "God Most High."[6]

While the people who lived in the early days of the earth knew of God and His sovereignty, power, and mercy, only a few are recorded as having walked with God. Abram is one of those few.

God appeared to Abram and revealed Himself as *El Shaddai* in Genesis 17:1. During this intimate interaction, God changed Abram's name to Abraham, which points to two things. First, the value God holds in a name—renaming Abram so that his name accurately aligned with who God made him to be. Second, El Shaddai points to the authority and specifics of God's nature to fulfill the promise He was releasing over Abraham.

Because the Hebrew language is so rich in meaning, El Shaddai can be defined accurately in several ways: "God of the Holy Mountain," "God of the Wilderness," "God the Destroyer of Enemies," "God the All-Sufficient One," "God the Nurturer of Babies (the Breasted One)," "God the Almighty," "the Sovereign God," or "the God who is more than enough."[7]

These descriptions of El Shaddai speak to the ways Abraham would need to trust in God as he continued in faith to receive the promise of a son through Sarah. God expanded Abraham's knowledge to enable him to know and grab hold of God's essence—His authority, to fulfill His promise.

Years later, Abraham came to know God as *Yahweh-jireh*, which means "Yahweh Appears" or "Yahweh Provides,"[8] when his dedication and obedience were tested. After asking him to sacrifice his promised son and seeing that Abraham would hold nothing back from Him, God appeared and provided a ram for the sacrifice instead.[9]

Abraham is an excellent example of growing in the knowledge of God and knowing His various names throughout life. His *knowing* deepened in each stage of his life as he chose to trust and obey regardless of what he was experiencing or the level of his understanding.

The names mentioned above are only a handful of those found in the Old Testament. There are many more, along with beautiful stories of how God revealed the different aspects of His nature and character to His children.

Freedom to Pursue

Just as God revealed Himself to Abraham, He also revealed Himself to Abraham's son, Isaac, and grandson Jacob. Knowing about God and the promises He made to them through Abraham wasn't enough. Both Isaac and Jacob needed their own personal encounters with God.

The same goes for us today. This is why I was determined to teach my children that they had to know God for themselves, not only through what they heard from me. This is also why I was overjoyed when my daughter spoke openly about her uncertainty. She wanted, and needed, to know Jesus personally.

Since the time my daughter announced her uncertainty as to whether or not she believed in God for herself, I have witnessed her heart knowledge grow. She has chosen to follow Jesus and His ways amidst a self-seeking culture. She listens to hear His voice above others, and her faith remains strong during challenges.

I have observed this process in each of my children—each having a journey of their own with various trials and growing in knowing Jesus with every experience. This process is how I have deepened and continue to deepen my intimacy with Him. And it's how you will too.

I believe all of us begin our journey to know God with some level of uncertainty and need. And quite honestly, we face those obstacles in different forms throughout our lives. But when we seek Jesus with an open and honest heart, He faithfully reveals Himself to us.

We see in the Gospels how Jesus often revealed Himself to people through their needs. The sick knew Him as Healer. To the hungry, He was Provider. Those tormented by demons came to know Him as Deliverer. He revealed Himself as Rescuer to the lost. For Matthew, a Jew hated by his people for collecting taxes for the Romans, Jesus was Restorer. To the dead, Jesus was Resurrection.

Jesus isn't only one thing to each person. He is all to all. For example, many of the people who received healing also ate the miraculous meals of multiplied fish and loaves. He was their healer and provider. We are able to embrace and take hold of more of who He is as we continue pursuing Him. Jesus allowed people freedom in their pursuit of knowing Him in greater ways. Many came to Him for what they could get—far less sought to know Him intimately by walking with Him daily. However, He longs to walk with us through life, revealing more of Himself along the way.

Regardless of how you have known Jesus thus far, you have the freedom to pursue Him more. He desires that the knowledge you have would propel you toward knowing Him more intimately. Isn't that wonderful? The deep in Him is calling out to the deep in you. Jesus is pursuing you!

Who Am I to You?

Learning the meaning of *name* and pondering the questions that Jesus asked His disciples in Matthew 16 provoked me to ponder further. After many years of being born again, I heard Jesus asking me, *"Who am I to you?"*

Much like I've watched my children do, I found myself sorting through what I had learned from others and my personal experiences. With guidance from Holy Spirit and the written Word, I began to see Jesus in much simpler and practical ways. There was no doubt in my mind that Jesus is the Son of God. What was stirring in my spirit, though, was a desire for deeper intimacy that would simplify my walk with Him, an intimacy that would impact me practically. Developing deeper intimacy is part of *embracing and taking hold of His Name,* and it causes our character and actions to emulate His.

I invite you to join in my pondering and meditate on Jesus' question: "Who am I to you?" To meditate is to engage in contemplation or reflection. Scripture tells us to meditate on God's Word. When we allow ourselves to meditate, ponder, or deliberately examine the depth of our hearts, we will likely find the answer to the posed question. In this case, we find answers (plural), for it is impossible for one name to describe or thoroughly portray all of who Jesus is.

As you explore the following pages, imagine Jesus sitting with you, just like He did with the disciples. While He is profoundly majestic, He is not complicated. Embrace His simplicity and practicality as you discover more of who Jesus is to you.

Points to Ponder

At this juncture in your journey, who do you say Jesus is to you?

Can you identify a specific area where you have knowledge of Jesus but lack intimacy with Him? Ask Holy Spirit how to grow in that area. What strategy did He give?

Are you able to identify with how Abraham grew in knowing different aspects of God as he walked with Him? List at least one way you have grown in knowing an aspect of God's nature as you have walked with Him.

Prayer of Embrace

Jesus, I acknowledge You as Almighty God. Thank You for anointing me with the Spirit of wisdom and revelation as I pursue knowing You more intimately. Guide me as I sort through head and heart knowledge. Give me eyes to see and ears to hear as I meditate on who You are to me. Expand my understanding as You reveal Yourself to me in simple and practical ways through my daily walk with You. Amen.

Chapter 3

The Building Blocks of Knowing Jesus

JESUS MADE A STATEMENT THAT HAS OFTEN CAPTIVATED MY thoughts. He said that not everyone who calls Him Lord will enter Heaven's Kingdom.[1] Even some who do great things in His name will be sent away because they are not joined to Him. Wouldn't it be awful to go about doing good, amazing, or even miraculous things in Jesus' name and get to the end of our lives and learn we were never joined to Him? Since this scenario is a possibility, we must know that we know that we know Jesus. For our relationship with Jesus to lead us into eternal life, it must be established on a few foundational building blocks.

As I mentioned previously, I grew up knowing about God and going to church semi-regularly. I knew the story of Jesus and believed it. Within the depths of my heart, I had a longing to do right. Yet, in that particular church setting, I never learned I could be joined to Jesus through a personal relationship with Him.

Once, when I was approximately ten years old, someone asked me if I was a Christian. I remember feeling the telltale heat of embarrassment spread throughout my body because I didn't know what it meant to be a Christian. I recall replying, "I believe in God," and from that day forward, I thought I was a Christian simply because I believed in God.

As a teen, I became aware of the need to receive Jesus as my personal Savior. Because this was a foreign concept, it took a couple of years before I yielded and asked Him to live in me. By God's goodness and grace, He faithfully drew me into a relationship with Him.

But what is it that creates a sure relationship with Jesus? What "ingredients" are needed to build a connection that will not end with Him turning us away as described in Matthew 7? The answer to this, I believe, is held within the following foundational building blocks.

Faith

Faith is the core component of a solid relationship with Jesus. Hebrews 11:6 tells us, "Without faith living within us it would be impossible to please God. For we come to God in faith knowing that he is real and that he rewards the faith of those who passionately seek him."

Jesus is our faith. He actually birthed faith within us and leads us forward in faith's perfection.[2] No one seeks God if they don't have faith in Him in the first place. It is faith living in us that causes us to believe He is real. Faith also activates the truth of Acts 4:12: "There is no one else who has the power to save us, for there is only one name to whom God has given authority by which we must experience salvation: the name of Jesus."

Why is Jesus' name the only name with the power to save us? Because it's the only name that has the authority of Almighty God embedded within it to release salvation. Remember, one of the meanings of "name" is *authority*, the power to influence or command, or to grant freedom.[3] We only experience salvation by the authority that is held within Jesus' name. Each person must respond in faith to this reality. So, we see that faith establishes the premise of knowing Jesus.

Consider again Jesus' rejection of those who claimed to know Him but who were never joined to Him. They must have had faith in Jesus. Why else would they go about doing what He had commissioned His disciples to do? How else would they have the power to do these things, if not in His name? And yet, Jesus gave a startling response, "Go away from me, you lawless rebels! I've never been joined to you!" (Matthew 7:23).

What?! How could they do these things yet not be joined to Him? I don't have the answer in full, but it seems they knew enough of Jesus to believe in and act on what is possible through Him and His name, but not enough to be joined to Him.

There are a few things that I have learned by studying Scripture and through my experience as a part of the body of Christ that could apply here: Only God knows the heart of man;[4] not everything is as it seems; and doing great exploits doesn't equate to *knowing* Jesus.

Son of the Living God

Faith in God's existence is the starting point of our journey to knowing Jesus. But the question may remain: "Why Jesus? Why did God ascribe power and authority to His name?" Jesus answers this in John 17:3: "Eternal life means to know and experience You as the only true God, and to know and experience Jesus Christ, as the Son whom you have sent."

This is the same truth Peter declared to Jesus in Matthew 16:16: "You are the Anointed One, the Son of the living God." This truth that Jesus revealed and Peter declared is what I consider the second building block in knowing Jesus: Jesus is God's Son.

Once our faith that God exists is established, the first name we must know Jesus by is the "Son of the Living God." We know this because of Jesus' response to Peter's declaration: "You are favored and privileged Simeon, son of Jonah! For you didn't discover this on your own, but my Father in heaven has supernaturally revealed it to you. I give you the name Peter, a stone. And this rock will be the bedrock foundation on which I will build my church" (Matthew 16:17–18).

Our revelation that Jesus is the Son of God establishes the foundation for Him to build heavenly realities within our hearts. It is our heavenly Father who supernaturally reveals to us that Jesus is the Son of God, the Anointed One. When we open our hearts to the reality that He exists, He bestows His favor upon us by revealing Himself to us.

Ultimately, to declare Jesus as the Son of God is to declare His equality to God. Thus, acknowledging that He is the only human capable of fulfilling the required sacrifice to redeem mankind from sin, making Him the Savior of the world.

Savior

This brings me to what I would consider building block number three. We must acknowledge and receive Jesus as our Savior. During a conversation with a religious leader named Nicodemus in John 3:1–21, Jesus revealed that He would be lifted up to be the Savior of the world.

Who Is Jesus to You?

The entire passage is full of powerful truths; however, I'd like to focus on verses 16–18:

> For here is the way God loved the world—he gave his only, unique Son as a gift. So now everyone who believes in him will never perish but experience everlasting life. God did not send his Son into the world to judge and condemn the world, but to be its Savior and rescue it! So now there is no longer any condemnation for those who believe in him, but the unbeliever already lives under condemnation because they do not believe in the name of the only Son of God.

Throughout most of my life, I've heard verse 16 quoted as a stand-alone verse. While it holds a truth that everyone needs to know, there are more truths to be understood along with it. The first I'd like to point out is in verse 17: Jesus didn't come to condemn the world.

"World" can seem ambiguous, so let's make it personal. The "world" includes me, you, and every other human who has ever existed. Jesus didn't come to earth to condemn us. Instead, He came to be our Savior and rescue us, which is the second truth to point out from this passage.

Why? What do we need rescuing from? It's a great question, and the answer is found in the latter part of verse 18: "The unbeliever already lives under condemnation because they do not believe in the name of the only Son of God."

Every human needs to be rescued from the condemnation of not believing in the name of Jesus. When we don't live in corresponding faith with His authority, His character, or the essence of who He is, we are condemned. When we don't live in His presence, we are living apart from Him. He came to reveal Himself in hopes that we might believe in Him. He desires for us to embrace Him and take hold of His name because He loves us and doesn't want an eternity without us.

The first part of verse 18 says, "So now there is no longer any condemnation for those who believe in him," which reiterates the beloved verse 16, which states, "Everyone who believes in him will never perish but experience everlasting life." Believing in Jesus is not a mental decision. It is a heart response to seeing our sinful state and trusting Jesus to save us. Doing so is the only way to receive eternal life.

In Greek, "savior" means "a deliverer," and the word used for salvation includes the meaning "deliverance." Both "savior" and "salvation" come from the word *sozo*. Aside from save and deliver, *sozo* further means to protect, heal, and make whole. Knowing Jesus as Savior is what rescues us from eternal condemnation. But the salvation He provides is for our time on earth as well.

In between believing in Jesus and entering our eternal dwelling place beyond the confines of earth, we are meant to live from the wholeness He provides. Here on earth, we are able to experience deliverance from evil and sinful habits, divine protection, preservation for His purpose, and healing and wellness in our body and mind, as well as in our relationships. As we yield to the inner leading of Holy Spirit, we grow in our experience of salvation and knowing our beautiful Savior.

Lord

Knowing Jesus as Lord is what I consider to be building block number four. This name comes from the Greek word *kyrios*. It means "supreme in authority ... and controller," and is used as a respectful title. A synonym for Lord is Master. Since Jesus doesn't force anyone to believe in or follow Him, knowing Him as Lord and Master is dependent on us yielding to His control and authority.

Typically, a person will not yield to another willingly unless they know it is for their greater good. This is why I believe knowing Jesus as Lord comes after salvation. We surrender to being transformed into His likeness, choosing to embrace His original intent and design for our lives while living in alignment with His ways.

Thinking of the Lord as a controller may cause an aversion for some because, in our world today, some people enjoy controlling others by way of manipulation or cruel treatment to serve their purposes. This is not how Jesus functions. As our Lord, He oversees our lives and directs us according to the purpose and plan we are destined for. He doesn't rule as a power monger, but instead as our loving Creator.

Jesus has good plans and purposes for us but has given us the choice to surrender to Him or not. In His mercy, He becomes our Savior, but true transformation in our hearts, minds, and lives comes only when we willingly yield our will to His lordship, seeking first His Kingdom and His righteousness.[5]

A Firm Foundation

As I have presented these building blocks, I hope you envision them laid side by side, interconnected, as a firm foundation by which to build a life joined with Jesus. Each one—Faith, Son of the Living God, Savior, and Lord—is a crucial element by which we know Him.

May we not be like those Jesus spoke of, who thought they were joined to Him because of the impressive things they accomplished. Instead, let us be people who go to God in faith, trust Jesus as Savior, and live our lives in total surrender to Him.

Without these established building blocks, a deeper knowing of Jesus is hindered. If we don't come to Him in faith, believing that He is God and the only one able to rescue us from sin and condemnation, then we cannot be joined to Him. If we aren't willing to yield to Him as our Lord, there isn't room for expansion in our relationship with Him.

If you recall, in chapter one, I shared how I was struggling with situations in my life that weren't changing. I was born again. I had faith in Jesus as the Son of God. However, I had hit a wall that created limitations in how I knew Him. While I was focused on speaking and praying His name to get some things accomplished, He was more concerned about me being joined to Him.

I had not allowed Him to be Lord in certain areas, and other areas still needed salvation. Remember, salvation is more than a change in our eternal destination. Salvation includes deliverance and healing while we are on earth. We must be careful not to limit the spaces and places we allow Jesus to access. Our hearts must be open to fully receive Him. Revelation 3:20 tells us that He stands at the door and knocks, which means He won't force His way into areas where we do not welcome Him.

Be assured that as soon as you invite Him into your heart, your situation, or your pain, He is there. With every step you take to draw near to Jesus, He responds by drawing nearer to you. Life is more fulfilling as we willingly yield, respond, and welcome Him in, as we *embrace and take hold of* Him in faith as the Son of the Living God, Savior, and Lord.

Points to Ponder

Which one of the names of Jesus stood out to you the most in this chapter? What element of it touched you?

Are each of the four building blocks firmly established in your heart? If there is an area of weakness, write out a Scripture to meditate on to strengthen your knowledge of that element.

Who Is Jesus to You?

List any areas of your heart or life that need further salvation or where you need to surrender to Jesus' Lordship. Ask Holy Spirit to highlight a Scripture for you to declare over that specific need.

Prayer of Embrace

> *Jesus, thank You for birthing faith within me and leading me to know You as the Son of the Living God. Thank You for clothing Yourself with humanity to become Savior of the world, cleansing me of sin, and rescuing me from eternal condemnation. Help me to willingly surrender every area of my life to You, my Lord and Master, so that I may fulfill the destiny You have planned for me, and always trust that Your ways are superior to the ways of this world. May I live my life in divine embrace with Your Name, taking hold of Your Name so that every word I speak and every good work I do is a praise and a glory unto You. Amen.*

Part Two

Explore

The Significance of His Name

Chapter 4

Master Designer and Creator

Everything God does has purpose and intention
behind that design. It is a master design, and every
little thing has its proper place and function.
—Aiden Wilson Tozer—

There's a Grand Designer behind everything.
Your life is not a result of random chance, fate, or luck.
There is a master plan.
—Rick Warren, *A Purpose Driven Life*—

HAVE YOU NOTICED HOW INCREASINGLY MORE PEOPLE SEEM TO struggle these days with a lack of self-worth? Sadly, many are unable to value themselves or their uniqueness. Maybe you can relate to some degree. Deep within the hearts of many are one or both of the following questions: "Why do I exist?" and "Why am I the way I am?" Each question exposes an uncertainty of purpose. To overcome this identity crisis, we must realize that every human is created and fashioned by design.

Engineers design and create buildings, software, vehicles, machinery, and so on. Fashion Designers design and create clothing. Artists of all kinds design and create using a plethora of mediums. These are just a few examples of how humans design and create based on internal inspiration, the inspiration of those commissioning them, or the specific needs and wants of consumers. Their creations bring enjoyment and enable the accomplishment of all types of tasks and goals around the globe.

Design is a key element that affects most industries in one way or another. Whether it be design for architecture, animation, household products, or clothing fashion, before anything is created, a design must be in place. The best designs come with thoughtful attention to the task or need at hand and how to accomplish or fulfill it. The best motivation for creativity is pleasure and passion for that which is being created. The solution to our identity crisis is a greater understanding of our creator's passion and pleasure toward us, His creation.

A Good Place to Start

Just as the familiar song from *The Sound of Music* tells us, the beginning is a very good place to start, so let's start at the very beginning! Genesis 1:1 tells us, "In the beginning God created the heavens and the earth."

In John 1:1–3 we learn that Jesus was there, in the beginning, creating: "In the beginning the Living Expression was already there. And the Living Expression was with God, yet fully God. They were together—face-to-face, in the very beginning. And through his creative inspiration this Living Expression made all things, for nothing has existence apart from him!"

And again in Colossians 1:15–16 (ESV), we learn that "He [Jesus] is the image of the invisible God, the firstborn of all creation. For by him all things were created ... all things were created through him and for him." Nothing exists apart from Jesus. He is the Living Expression of Yahweh God and the creator of all things. Jesus is our starting point.

Fashioned and Formed

In Hebrew, the word bara is the root word for both "created" and "creator." It means to create by fashioning and shaping, according to personal selection and choice. In Genesis chapter one, God is the one shaping, fashioning, and creating the heavens and earth and everything in it.

All of creation is full of God's majesty and testifies to His creativity, nature, and character. You and I are a part of His majestic creation, for the Bible says, "The LORD God formed the man from the dust of the ground. He breathed the breath of life into the man's nostrils, and the man became a living person" (Genesis 2:7 NLT). Perhaps, the most beautiful aspect of being human is that we are made in God's image: "So God created human beings in his own image. In the image of God he created them; male and female he created them" (Genesis 1:27 NLT).

God is spirit, so we are spirit. He clothed us with an earthen body, creatively expressing the attributes of His nature and character through both the male and female forms. The word "formed" in Genesis 2:7 means to form or fashion in the same way a potter forms and fashions clay. It means to shape something according to its intended design to fulfill the intended purpose.

Our form is no mistake.

The Greek word for "created" means to fabricate or form originally. We were created through Jesus and for Jesus. He fabricated or constructed our human body from the dust of the earth. Since the first man, Adam, He has continued to form each one of us as an original. David testified to this truth in Psalm 139:13–16:

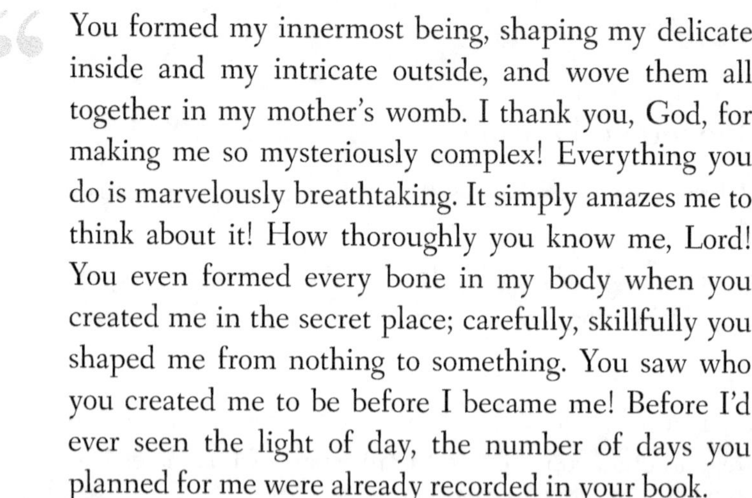

> You formed my innermost being, shaping my delicate inside and my intricate outside, and wove them all together in my mother's womb. I thank you, God, for making me so mysteriously complex! Everything you do is marvelously breathtaking. It simply amazes me to think about it! How thoroughly you know me, Lord! You even formed every bone in my body when you created me in the secret place; carefully, skillfully you shaped me from nothing to something. You saw who you created me to be before I became me! Before I'd ever seen the light of day, the number of days you planned for me were already recorded in your book.

Too many of us do not realize how intricately God has fashioned us. From our freckles and dimples to the color of our skin, hair, and eyes; from our height and shape to our personality and cute quirks; and from the natural skills we possess to our desire to be valuable, to have a voice, to play a part, and to make a difference—all of these characteristics express the creativity and attributes of our Creator.

Our unique design ought to be celebrated! We have been fashioned in God's image. God Almighty formed us and shaped us from nothing into the mysteriously complex human beings that we are—through and for Jesus. He creatively fashioned us with love and from love—after all, He *is* love.[1] He did so because He takes great delight and pleasure in us and designed each of us for a specific purpose.

Designed with Purpose

We can easily get caught in the trap of an identity crisis of not knowing who we are because we haven't been taught *whose* we are and what our true origin is. God specifically designed us according to His thoughtful intention. As we yield our lives to Him, He reveals our purpose, and we fulfill the destiny He fashioned for us. Paul spoke of this truth in Ephesians 2:10, saying, "We have become his poetry, a re-created people that will fulfill the destiny he has given each of us, for we are joined to Jesus, the Anointed One. Even before we were born, God planned in advance our destiny and the good works we would do to fulfill it!"

This verse teaches us that not one human is born by happenstance or mistake. Nor are we made on an assembly line that prints out exact replicas. Each of us is skillfully formed within the womb of our mother. No matter the intentions or "un-intentions" of our earthly parents, Jesus created us with a plan. Together with Him, we are destined for good and to bring forth good.

Even during times of trouble, our destiny and purpose remain steadfast. The challenges we face while on earth do not override the plan of God. We see this truth illustrated beautifully during a painful period in the history of the Jewish nation. When the people of Israel had been taken into captivity for a set time, God spoke encouragement through the prophet Jeremiah. The same words God spoke to His people then, He still speaks to each of us who embrace Him now.

 Here's what Yahweh says to you: "I know all about the marvelous destiny I have in store for you, a future planned out in detail. My intention is not to harm you but to surround you with peace and prosperity and to give you a beautiful future, glistening with hope. When you call on me and come to me in prayer, I will listen to your every word. If you reach out to me, you will find me when you search for me with all your heart. I will not disappoint you," declares Yahweh. "All that you have lost, I will restore."

— Jeremiah 29:11–14

With these truths, we are equipped and empowered to rebel against the lies of the enemy that come at us through modern culture, the opinions of those around us, or the pain and trauma we have experienced. We can combat the lies that tell us we have no value, and we aren't good enough—lies that create confusion about our identity.

These lies and many more cause despair and can send us reeling in search of significance and purpose. These lies lead us away from what we were created for and who we were created to be.

Created for Glory

Hundreds of years before God came to earth, clothed in human form, He answered our question, "Why do I exist?" through His prophet Isaiah. Within His answer lies the truth of our worth and our divine purpose: "Bring me everyone who is called by my name, the ones I created to experience my glory. I myself formed them to be who they are and made them for my glory" (Isaiah 43:7).

We exist—as He formed us—for His glory! We also "become like mirrors who brightly reflect the glory of the Lord Jesus" (2 Corinthians 3:18). Each one of us was fashioned with delight, pleasure, and passion to experience His glory. Designed specifically and uniquely, we aren't meant to conform to the image of others or culture. We may seem an unlikely choice to those around us, yet in the hands of a Master Designer, we are exactly what is needed to fulfill His purpose.

In times of uncertainty, you can be certain that you are not a mistake. You have been created for an eternal purpose full of good and hope. Each of us has gifts and talents that God intends us to use to bring forth joy for ourselves and those around us. We are valuable and full of worth. While our purposes vary, each of us has been designed, created, and fashioned for glory.

Accepting and embracing who God made us to be empowers us to live free from lies and doubts about our true value. Ultimately, as we open our hearts to *embrace* Jesus as our Master Designer and Creator, we experience the pleasure He has had in us from "the very beginning."

Points to Ponder

Are you able to identify any lies that have caused you to struggle with a lack of self-worth? List them here.

List one specific way you have been fashioned uniquely. What makes you special?

Ask Jesus to reveal how your unique design relates to your unique purpose. What did He say?

Prayer of Embrace

Jesus, forgive me for believing and aligning with the lie(s) sent to deter me from knowing You, my purpose, and Your glory. I acknowledge, accept, and embrace the reality that You have masterfully created and designed me to be who I am. Help me to overcome all uncertainties I have struggled with as I shift my mindset to believe that You fashioned me with passion and love, and that I bring You pleasure. I open my heart to experience Your glory and reflect it to the world around me. Amen.

Chapter 5

Redeemer

For I know that my Redeemer and Vindicator lives,
And at the last He will take His stand upon the earth.
—Job 19:25 AMP—

There is only one relationship that matters,
and that is your personal relationship to a personal
Redeemer and Lord. Let everything else go,
but maintain that at all cost, and God will fulfill
His purpose through your life."
—Oswald Chambers—

REDEEMER. THIS IS ONE OF THE MOST IMPORTANT NAMES TO know Jesus by. Jesus, our redeemer, took the punishment for our sins on the cross, and we are forgiven by His shed blood. With a deeper understanding of what He accomplished for us on the cross, what it is to be redeemed, and why we need redemption, we can more fully embrace Jesus as our wonderful, majestic, loving Redeemer.

An Up-Close Look Into the Meaning of Redeemer

Years ago, at that little white church mentioned in chapter one, I sat gazing upon the many paintings that decorated the front wall of the sanctuary. Each one stated a name or attribute of Jesus. On this particular day, my eyes became fixed on the painting that read "Redeemer." After a few minutes, in my mind's eye, I saw it hyphenated: Re-deem-er. I began to analyze the word with the prefix *re* and the suffix *er*. I understood *re* to mean again, and *deem* means to judge or have an opinion.[1] Our judgments reveal the value we place on people and things. While this isn't the definition of "redeemer," God spoke this unique message to my heart that day to bring a deeper revelation of who He is as our redeemer, one who judges again or "re-judges" us.

In the Hebrew language, redeemer means "to be the next of kin," the one who would buy back a relative's property or marry his widow. This is foreign to our modern-day culture in the US. However, in ancient times, if a man became bankrupt, it was expected that his closest relative would redeem him by purchasing his property to keep it in the family.

Also foreign to Americans is the concept that women in ancient times were utterly dependent on their husbands and became destitute if their husbands died. It was necessary for a relative to redeem the widow by marrying her and caring for her needs. In both these acts of redemption, the relative was making a "judgment again" of their worth.

A great example of redeeming is found in the book of Ruth. After moving from Bethlehem to Moab due to famine, Elimelech and Naomi's two sons married Moabite women, one of whom was Ruth. Eventually, Elimelech and both his sons died, leaving three widows. Naomi sent her daughter-in-laws back to their families, but Ruth refused to leave Naomi and instead, returned to Bethlehem with her.

I am leaving some details out, but in the end, both women were redeemed by Naomi's kinsman-redeemer, Boaz, who married Ruth. He deemed both Naomi and Ruth valuable and brought them back into the family.

Jesus became human so that He could be our Kinsman-Redeemer. He is the only one able to re-establish our worth, according to God's original intent and design. Genesis 1 tells us that *all* that God made was good and not evil. So, you may wonder, why is there still evil plaguing the earth? Why does God allow evil? These are valid questions.

Over the years, I have walked with people through loss, trauma, and tragedy and have had plenty of my own. Life trials can be heart-wrenching. After a conversation with a loved one regarding such things, I spent several days seeking the Lord for revelation in this matter. I had been wondering for years, but this time I held these questions before Him without relent. I wanted to understand.

The Story of Esther

In my pondering, Esther continued to come to mind. After several days, I heard in my spirit, *"The king's decree cannot be revoked."* I remember sitting for a while, hearing this phrase on repeat, and being led to the book of Esther.

In Esther 3, we see how an evil man, Haman, who hated the Jews, concocted a plan and deceived the king into ridding the region of them. With permission to use the king's signet ring, Haman issued a decree for the destruction of all Jews. When the plan was found out, Esther risked her life to go before the king and intercede for her people.[2] Ultimately, after revealing Haman's plan to wipe out her people, he was hanged on the gallows he had built for the Jews.[3] The man behind the plan was gone, but the decree he had formulated was still active.

Esther then asked the king to revoke the decree Haman had created, but the king explained he could not go against his own decree.[4] However, he gave his signet ring to Mordecai and Esther to create a decree that would supersede the one written by Haman, and they did just that. The new decree stated that each Jew was able to take up defenses and kill anyone who would try to kill them. The day came, and the Jews were delivered because vengeance came upon anyone who sought to harm them.

Back to the Beginning

As I read through the story of Esther, I continued to hear *"The king's decree cannot be revoked,"* and the six days of creation came to mind. The Lord opened my understanding: Everything He spoke in the beginning was a decree. Each one of those decrees was fulfilled and has continued because they cannot be revoked.

After creating Adam in His image as the prototype for all mankind, God made some decrees. He gave Adam and all mankind dominion over the Earth. By commissioning Adam and Eve to be fruitful and multiply, He made a decree for them and all generations to follow, to produce more humans.[5]

It was never God's intention or desire for evil to dwell among or within man. He intended that mankind would live in intimate union with Him, enjoying the fruit of many trees in the Garden, along with the Tree of Life. However, He also desired mankind to reciprocate His love, which means the power to choose had to be given.

To provide choice, God also placed the Tree of the Knowledge of Good and Evil in the Garden and explained that they must not eat from it, or they would die. Genesis 3 tells how Satan deceived Eve into eating fruit from this tree, disobeying God's instructions. When Adam and Eve consumed the fruit of that tree, the knowledge of evil entered them. It became a part of their DNA, and every human since has been born with a sin nature, knowing good and evil. Along with the knowledge of evil, death became part of the human experience on earth.

God established free will in the Garden, and because His decrees are eternal, every human has the choice to partner with good or evil. Unfortunately, this allows humans to hurt others who are in their sphere of influence, even those who are innocent and undeserving of evil treatment. Because He is all-knowing, God saw the need for redemption before the foundation of the world and established a plan to rescue us from all that is less than the glory He destined us for.

The Parallel Between Esther and the Story of Creation

The words I heard from Holy Spirit were the words of King Xerxes in Esther 8:8: "Now write another decree in the king's name in behalf of the Jews as seems best to you, and seal it with the king's signet ring *—for no document written in the king's name and sealed with his ring can be revoked*" (emphasis added). A King's decree cannot be revoked. In our modern day, kings and leaders seem to go against their word regularly and seemingly think nothing about it. Not so with God.

Esther's story reveals God's redemption for all humanity. Haman hated the Jews and sought to destroy them. In the same way, Satan hates and seeks to destroy God's image bearers. King Xerxes represents Adam, the one who had dominion and was deceived into handing over his authority. Esther represents Jesus; she made intercession to save her people, and the edict that Esther and Mordecai wrote represents God's plan from before the foundation of the earth.

God's decree, His spoken words to Adam in the beginning, couldn't be revoked. He had given him authority, dominion, and free will to choose and wouldn't go back on His word. Neither would He revoke

His decree to multiply, so, unfortunately, Adam's choice to partake of the knowledge of evil affected every human after him. While this could seem hopeless, it is not!

God's Higher Decree

Before He ever spoke a word, God knew mankind would fall, so He established salvation through life union with Jesus to supersede evil. He was slain from before the foundation of the world[6] to redeem mankind, and through the course of time, Jesus manifested God's decree on earth.

He clothed Himself with humanity, suffered in all ways as we do, yet never sinned. Jesus carried our sins and the sins committed against us to the cross, saving us from the condemnation brought upon us by Adam's choice. He shed His blood and died a criminal's death in our place.[7]

Adam and Eve's choice placed humanity in captivity under Satan's dominion, and Jesus' blood paid the ransom. He bought us back and set us free.[8] None of us could have ever paid the debt or canceled our wrongs, but His blood did. Jesus freed us from the eternal consequences of sin, and instead of condemnation, He offers eternal life to those who embrace Him and take hold of His *name*.

Living Redeemed

Living as one redeemed by Jesus means much more than praying a "sinner's prayer" and being forgiven; it involves a deeper commitment to Him. When we receive the blood of Jesus to redeem us, we exchange our sin nature for His holiness. He has judged us again through His blood and no longer condemns us. We are "re-deemed" by God's decree: forgiven, righteous, and holy.

The effects of sin and death lose their power when we receive the blood of Jesus to replace our own. As we transform into His image, the desire to sin, along with the effect and stain from our sins, is removed. In addition, we are cleansed from the sins committed against us. In Christ, death has no power because when our earthly bodies die, our spirits are immediately in the presence of God for eternity. While we remain on earth, we are also redeemed from the death experienced in our souls due to hurt, pain, and wickedness.

Through the shed blood of Jesus, we have been given access to live from the higher decree of His righteousness. By sharing in His crucifixion, we share in His resurrection and have the power of Holy Spirit within us to overrule the evil of this natural world. Jesus not only secured eternal life for us, but His blood also brings judgment. We are not guilty! Instead, we are empowered to live unquestionably free!

Just as Haman demonstrated, Satan seeks to kill, steal, and destroy.[9] On earth, we face evil because Satan remains the ruler of the earthly realm.[10] However, in Christ, we have overcome this temporal world and live in His Kingdom reality: abundant life, life above and beyond what we experience without Him.[11]

As Christ's re-deemed ones, we are once again judged to have dominion on the earth. He has positioned us in Himself and delegated us to rule and reign with Him, just as God had initially given Adam authority to do. We are to rule over evil with good, just like Jesus did, bringing the Kingdom of Heaven to earth.

These truths do not minimize the pain suffered here on earth or the struggles we face. They do, however, empower us to overcome evil and its effects. God tells us in Isaiah 55:9, "As high as the heavens are above the earth, so my ways and my thoughts are higher than yours." God's ways and thoughts are revealed to us in Scripture by the inspiration of Holy Spirit. His Word is our armor and the weapon we war with.

Whatever we may face here on earth, there is a higher reality for us to grab hold of. Jesus demonstrated for us how to live according to the Kingdom of Heaven while on earth. When tempted by Satan, Jesus overcame him by speaking the Word of God.[12] When the Pharisees and Sadducees attempted to ensnare Him, He spoke eternal truths. They hurled accusations at Him and made efforts to kill Him before His assignment was complete. We know Jesus experienced extreme physical agony, but imagine His emotional suffering due to rejection, doubt, and unbelief.

Through it all, He loved. He endured the cross with joy because He knew the reality of Heaven's Kingdom and that the ransom He was paying meant we could be one with Him again. In the Garden, mankind was judged as separated from God because of choosing evil. Through the cross and blood of Jesus, mankind has been redeemed, judged as righteous again, *if* we choose to accept His redemption.

In the story of Ruth, Naomi had to choose to return to the land she came from to receive redemption. We, too, need to return to the "land" we came from—God. Receiving redemption means we receive God's higher decree over our lives—Jesus. This includes every part of our lives. We must let go of anything we have partnered with that doesn't align with God's decree of righteousness and all the wrongs we have experienced from others.

Forgiveness is foundational concerning redemption. We must receive forgiveness from Jesus and then extend His forgiveness to others. Forgiving our offenders doesn't excuse their actions; it sets us free.

Along with forgiving others, we need to forgive ourselves. Jesus redeemed us through an act of forgiveness, not holding our sins against us; we must do the same. There may also be a need to let go of the offense we hold in our heart toward God. If we felt like He let us down or abandoned us, we must receive His healing and truth concerning that lie.

This is challenging, to say the least, because the pain is real, and in no way do I want to minimize the agony suffered. I do, however, desire for you to be free from the pain that grips your soul. As you surrender your pain to Jesus, He is faithful to redeem you, bringing healing and freedom in exchange for every burden laid down. He is trustworthy, and He promises to be faithful to His Word.[13]

When we bow our knees to Jesus, we must lay down all the burdens we have been carrying. The evil that entered our earthen vessels in the Garden brought pain and sorrow. Jesus, who is pure love clothed with earth, brings healing. He is the Living Word[14] and all truths and promises recorded in Scripture hold power to manifest His love in our lives. The reality of His Word is the reality He has for us...now, on earth. His Word is the higher decree for us to war with, just like Esther and Mordecai's edict empowered the Jews to overcome Haman's evil intentions.

It is important to note that even though evil often comes at us through people, we aren't fighting people. Our true fight is against principalities and powers of darkness that influence people.[15] The most powerful way to war against evil is with the Word of God. We can overcome the evil we experience by grabbing hold of the promises of the good that God intends for us. By searching the truths of Scripture that speak specifically to our situations, we can create a prayer of declaration to war with, declaring God's Word until we see the truth manifest.

Eternal redemption is secured by the blood of Jesus for all who will receive Him. Not only are all the sins we have committed and endured washed away, but we are also set free from the sin nature. In addition to eternal life, His blood has secured abundant life for us now. We have been judged righteous again; we are redeemed, bought back, and set free to live empowered by His higher decree.

We must be like Esther and Mordecai and not surrender to the enemy as he seeks to destroy. Instead, we must pursue freedom by aligning ourselves with God's higher decree: life over death, good over evil. By refusing evil in our lives and partnering with the Word of God by decreeing His reality over our lives and situations, we *embrace and take hold of* Jesus as our Redeemer.

Points to Ponder

What spoke to you the most in this chapter?

What area of your life needs to experience Jesus Christ's higher decree?

Ask Holy Spirit to highlight one or two Scriptures for you to decree over your life and specific situations you may be facing. Write them here.

Prayer of Embrace

Jesus, thank You for loving me so much that You came to redeem me from my captivity. Thank You for paying the ransom and setting me free. Help me to identify areas in my life where I need to apply the cleansing power of your blood and the reality of the redemption you provided for me. I refuse to partner with evil, but instead, I will overcome it by aligning with Your goodness. I choose to live righteously, according to Your higher decree. Lead me as I pursue Your abundant life on earth, embracing You as my Redeemer. Amen.

Chapter 6

A Friend Like No Other

The dearest friend on earth is
a mere shadow compared to Jesus Christ.
—Oswald Chambers,
Studies in the Sermon on the Mount—

A rule I have had for years is: to treat
the Lord Jesus Christ as a personal friend.
His is not a creed, a mere doctrine,
but it is He Himself we have.
—Dwight L. Moody, *New Sermons*—

WHAT IS IT TO BE A FRIEND? THE MEANING OF THE WORD CAN be relative and vague from one person's perspective to another. It seems there are varying depths to the term as well. It is used by some as a loose greeting for an acquaintance, while others use it only for those whom they trust with their deepest secrets. I appreciate and honor both of these approaches and the reasoning behind them. However, such a variance in the term friend can create a lack of certainty when relating to Jesus as our friend. When Jesus called His disciples friends, was He just being kind, or was there a deep connection between them? By the end of this chapter, we will see the reality of what friendship with Jesus holds for each one of us.

I've had many good friends through the years. As good as those friends have been, each of them has only walked with me for a season of my life. While each one has known some of my heart, none has known all the intimate details.

Within those friendships, I have also experienced some difficulties. One in particular caused a deep sense of rejection. The rejection I felt stung severely. My heart was broken and swirling with confusion. I didn't understand the reasoning behind the rejection, but I understood the pain.

There was a moment when I was crying out to God, and I heard Jesus say, "Let Me be your best friend." I remember how surprised I was to hear Him say this. I was even more surprised at the honest response that bubbled up from my heart. With desperation, I replied, "I don't know how."

What Is a Friend?

When it comes to words that I understand contextually, I don't often investigate the definition because, well, I understand it. However, when I'm prompted to look up the meaning, as I was with the word *name*, I am often surprised to find there is more to the meaning than I realized. Friend is one of those words.

Merriam-Webster defines a friend as "one attached to another by affection or esteem; a favored companion."[1] This is in line with Isaiah 41:8, where it is written that God spoke of Abraham as His friend. The Hebrew word used for "friend" in that passage is *ahab*, and its simplest meanings are "to love," "to have affection for," and "friend."

Ahab is used 169 times for "love" and twelve times for "friend." When used for a friend, it implies an intimacy beyond that of a companion; it describes one who is loving and beloved. What this tells me is that when God names someone His friend, it is more than a kind greeting. He is bestowing His mark of love and deep, intimate affection upon that person. A friendship such as this isn't surface-level or casual.

Ahab is the word used in 1 Samuel 18:1: "The soul of Jonathan was knit to the soul of David, and Jonathan loved [ahab] him as his own soul" (ESV). The depth of Jonathan's love for his friend was demonstrated a few verses later as he "stripped himself of the robe that was on him and gave it to David, and his armor, and even his sword and his bow and his belt" (18:4 ESV). This wasn't simply a kind gesture; by doing this, Jonathan gave his position in Saul's kingdom to David. What love! Although Jesus didn't give up His position as Son of God, this is exactly what He did for us when "he emptied himself of his outward glory by reducing himself to the form of a lowly servant" (Philippians 2:7).

Earthly friendships typically start at the surface and deepen by spending time in one another's presence. By walking together on life's path, we learn to value our friends' strengths and support their weaknesses.

In our friendship with Jesus, we start at the surface and spend our journey with Him learning how magnificent He is. He, on the other hand, knows all about us. He knows our weaknesses and strengths alike and is full of love and intimate affection for us. Even while we were still stuck in sin, He took our penalty upon Himself and laid down His life.

Love like this is foreign—literally, not of this world. Jesus came to demonstrate love from the Kingdom of Heaven and teach His disciples to do the same. We read of one such teaching in John 15:12–15:

Love each other deeply, as much as I have loved you. For the greatest love of all is a love that sacrifices all. And this great love is demonstrated when a person sacrifices his life for his friends. You show that you are my intimate friends when you obey all that I command you. I have never called you 'servants,' because a master doesn't confide in his servants, and servants don't always understand what the master is doing. But I call you my most intimate and cherished friends, for I reveal to you everything that I've heard from my Father.

Although they had not yet seen the fullness of His love through His sacrifice on the cross, they had experienced His deep affection for them. He had placed value upon them by calling "them to be continually at his side as his friends" (Mark 3:14), and they witnessed Him giving of Himself relentlessly to them and others, even when tired, hungry, and harassed.

This command to love the way Jesus loved them was no small thing. Intimate friendship compels us to do hard things, knowing that the reward is greater than the cost. Laying our lives down for our friend, Jesus, is illustrated through our obedience to His commands and His teachings—His Word. Laying down our lives for our other friends is the fulfillment of one of those commands and can look a myriad of ways. Whatever the specifics, love is the driving force.

Never a Servant

I find it interesting that Jesus highlighted the contrast between the relationships of master and servant versus that of the affectionate love between intimate friends. It seems He identified a heart issue within His disciples, a struggle with a slave mindset. In His last hours with

His disciples, He clearly communicated that they were His friends, not servants.

Most translations use the Greek text in verse 15: "I will *no longer* call you servants." The Passion Translation uses the Aramaic: "I *have never* called you 'servants'" (emphasis added). Jesus spoke Aramaic. He pointed out that masters don't share secrets with their slaves. Therefore, He couldn't have considered them as such, since He had revealed to them everything He had heard from His Father. He still shares His secrets with His friends, with us, as we spend time in His presence in the secret place and in His Word.

Another point Jesus could have made is that masters didn't usually lay down their lives for a servant; rather, servants laid their lives down daily for their masters. Instead, He told them that "great love is demonstrated when a person sacrifices his life for his friends" (John 15:13). Before they understood the lengths to which Jesus would go to demonstrate His love for them, He was drawing them into the reality of friendship with Him, in which love was the root.

Jesus is Lord and Master over all the universe and those of us who willingly lay down our lives to serve His purpose. However, His desire is that we do so from a deep, loving friendship, not as a servant. All but one of the twelve disciples eventually became apostles, establishing the Kingdom of Heaven wherever they went, but first, they were His *most intimate and cherished friends.*

Sons, Not Servants

The word for servant in Greek is *doulos,* and in Aramaic it is *avada.*[2] In English, these words are translated as "slave" or "bond-servant." Obedience and labor are forced upon a slave, whereas a bond-servant loves their master and chooses to serve willingly. While we willingly serve the purposes of God out of our love for Him, Jesus specified that He doesn't see us as servants, but as friends.

Since Jesus spoke Aramaic, the Aramaic word *racham* would've been what He used for "most intimate and cherished friend," and it would've caused a shift in His disciples' thinking. *Racham* denotes the highest possible position that someone can hold in a relationship; it is the very child from the womb of its mother.[3] Jesus was calling the disciples actual family members who came from the womb of God.

Calling His disciples *racham* is in alignment with John 1:12: "But those who embraced Him and took hold of His name, He gave authority to become the children of God!" His friendship with them, and with all of us who embrace Him, is born from intimacy, birthed from the womb of God. Our friendship with Jesus is the deepest, most intimate friendship we could ever have. He doesn't want servants; He wants brothers and sisters living in and from friendship with Him.

With this understanding, Proverbs 17:17 takes on deeper meaning: "A dear friend will love you no matter what, and a family sticks together through all kinds of trouble." Jesus is indeed that friend who will love you no matter what. And being born from the womb of God, we are in His family. God the Father is our father. Jesus is our brother. Our spirit is mingled with Holy Spirit. There is no separating us from Him, and no amount of trouble can separate us from His love. As His family, His friendship with us doesn't waver or fade, and He doesn't get disappointed.

The love of a dear friend, as stated in the verse above, is the Hebrew word *ahab* (defined at the beginning of this chapter). It implies an intimacy beyond companionship. It can also mean to desire, breathe after, or long for another. Jesus is more than a friend in terms of how we may be accustomed to friendship. He breathes fresh breath from Heaven into us, and we, in turn, give our breath to proclaim His name.

Friendship with Jesus

One might think that friendship with Jesus is earned because of His words: "You show that you are my intimate friends when you obey all that I command you" (John 15:14). In actuality, our obedience simply comes from *being* friends. After being in His presence, His disciples longed to follow His instructions. The same is true for us. As His disciples, we love Him and want to live in alignment with His heart and establish His Kingdom and purposes on earth as it is in Heaven. As intimate friends, we hear His truths and secrets and experience many blessings that come from His Kingdom realm.

Jesus is the friend who loves at all times and always stays close. Even when Peter denied Him, Jesus forgave and restored him. He doesn't only love us when it's convenient or when our actions benefit Him. Jesus loves us and remains our friend, whether:

- We get things right or we stumble and make mistakes
- We are at our best or at our worst
- We understand or we don't
- We are strong or we are weak
- We are faithful to Him or we aren't
- We seek Him or we don't

Learning to depend on Jesus as my best friend proved to be quite a challenge for me. I had a hard time understanding how He could possibly want to be my closest companion. The times I had experienced rejection throughout life created within me a belief that I wasn't likable or wanted for who I was. Without realizing it, I viewed my relationship with Jesus through the lens of performance. I had no problem serving Him, doing whatever I could to please Him. But deep down, I wasn't confident that He loved or wanted me for who I was. I needed to *know* Jesus as my friend, yet subconsciously I feared He would reject me like others had.

Often, I would hear Him whisper truths of His love to my heart, but believing Him didn't come easily. I was prone to believe the lies that had found residence in my soul. At times, I would seek consolation and affirmation from another person, but no human friend could fill the void of the intimate friendship I desired.

Friendship with Jesus is a lifelong journey. Each step of the way, He proves to be that friend who loves no matter what and stays through all sorts of trouble. There is nothing we can do to make Him love us more, and there is nothing we can do to cause Him to love us less. No one else could ever offer a better friendship than Jesus. May we reciprocate His friendship by sacrificing our lives for Him, faithfully obeying His commands, and *embracing and taking hold of* Him as our most intimate and cherished Friend. A friend like no other.

Points to Ponder

- Would you say your friendship with Jesus has been casual or intimate up to this point?
- What stood out the most to you about the depths of intimacy available in your friendship with Jesus?

Prayer of Embrace

Jesus, You call me to Your side as a friend. Draw me closer to You, and deepen my affection for You and my connection to You. Anoint my heart to receive revelation of the magnitude of Your tender love for me. Anoint my ears to hear the secrets of the Kingdom which You desire to share with me as I walk close to You. Thank You, Jesus, for being my friend. Amen.

Chapter 7

The Good Shepherd

I myself will be the shepherd of my sheep, and I will give
them rest. I will seek out the lost one, bring back the stray,
bandage the injured, and heal those that are sick. I will watch
over the fat and healthy of the flock. I will be a true, caring
shepherd to them. I, Lord Yahweh, have spoken.
—Ezekiel 34:15—

Let us only take heed that this office of Christ is not
set before us in vain. It will profit us nothing at
the last day that Jesus was a Shepherd, if during our
lifetime, we never heard His voice and followed Him.
If we love life, let us join His flock without delay.
**—J.C. Ryle, *Expository Thoughts on the
Gospels*—**

A true shepherd leads the way.
He does not merely point the way.
—Leonard Ravenhill—

ONE MORNING AS I SAT WITH THE LORD, I HEARD HIM SAY, "*I am the Good Shepherd; regardless of the terrain we tread, I am good. I am present, and I walk with you over the terrain. I am with you in the circumstances. I am good. My rod and My staff, they comfort you... I AM the Good Shepherd.*"

The truth that He is my Shepherd was something I really needed to be reminded of at that time. I also needed the reassurance that He is always with me, no matter the terrain or the circumstances.

In John 10:11 and 14, Jesus names Himself as the Good Shepherd, but how many of us actually understand what that means or entails? In our modern day, the ways a shepherd cares for his sheep aren't well known. It's likely that most of us are limited to the image of someone standing in a field watching over sheep with a curved staff in hand. By gaining a practical understanding of the role of a shepherd, we can *embrace and take hold of* Jesus as our Good Shepherd.

David introduced God as our shepherd long before Jesus spoke of Himself as our Good Shepherd. A footnote for Psalm 23:1 reveals the heart of a shepherd: "The unique term for shepherd is *ro'eh tzon*-'lover of the flock.' This teaches us that a shepherd was not just a responsible overseer, but a caring father figure, tending to his flock out of a deep sense of love. Shepherds were also fierce protectors of their flocks."[1]

Doesn't that bring a deeper sense of comfort? Shepherds have an affection for their flock. In fact, the few people I know who have raised sheep say how easy it is to get attached to them.

Jesus doesn't shepherd us simply as an occupation or out of obligation. He tends to us out of the deepest love there is, a love that is eternal and far beyond what we understand. He is our fierce protector.

Tools of the Trade

In ancient times, shepherds used a few specific tools to protect their flocks: a rod, a staff, a sling, and their voice. I will cover the shepherd's staff in the next chapter; for now, let's look at the first three.

The Rod

In Psalm 23:4 (NIV), David wrote, "Even though I walk through the darkest valley, I will fear no evil, for you are with me; your rod and your staff, they comfort me." The Hebrew word for rod here is *sebet*. It comes from an unused root, probably meaning to branch off.

In my research, I learned that when a shepherd's son was old enough to help care for the sheep, he would search for a choice sapling and dig it from the ground. The enlarged base where the trunk joined the root was whittled down slowly and accurately into a smooth, rounded head of hard wood.

After shaping the sapling to fit his hand perfectly, the young shepherd spent many hours throwing the rod to acquire speed and accuracy for hitting a target. Once these skills were mastered, the rod became his most powerful weapon of defense for himself and the sheep, and he was never without it. With his skillful accuracy, the shepherd could throw the rod to the far side of a wandering sheep or one nearing danger to startle it and cause it to return to the flock.

Within the word *sebet*, there is also the literal meaning of a stick that would be used for punishing and fighting; however, the shepherd would never impose harm on his flock with his hand-tailored rod. Instead, he would use it to "punish" or fight off large predators such as coyotes and wolves. He would beat bushes to scare off small creatures and snakes possibly lurking within the branches and posing a threat. With such strong defense capabilities, the shepherd's rod provided a deep sense of comfort for himself and the sheep.

Another meaning of the word *sebet* is a scion, which is a young shoot of a plant, a twig cut for grafting. It can also mean a descendant of a notable family.[2] This definition takes us deeper into the mystery of God. Evidently, in Psalm 23, when David says he is comforted by the rod of God, he is speaking prophetically of the "shoot"[3] of God. Jesus was the very rod, or scion, that would come from David's family line, "grafted" into the earth realm from Heaven within the womb of a virgin, establishing the royal Kingdom of God on earth. Amazing.

David's secret-place intimacy with God yielded deep understanding far beneath the surface. He heard and declared the very secrets God only shares with His lovers.

The Sling

The shepherd's sling was also instrumental in caring for the flock. With a couple of swings, he could accurately launch a stone against thieves and predatory animals or startle a straying sheep back toward the flock.[4] Within the story of David and Goliath, we see how accurate a shepherd could be with his sling. Goliath would have been wearing a helmet that not only covered his head but most of his face as well. David's accuracy landed that smooth stone right between Goliath's eyes, killing him with one powerful blow.

His Voice

At night, out in the open fields, shepherds would gather with their flocks. Finding safety at watchtowers or in caves, the shepherds would take turns keeping watch throughout the night. When morning came, each shepherd would call for their sheep, using yet another tool: his voice.

There was no confusion as to which sheep belonged to which shepherd because each sheep recognized the voice of its shepherd. Whether by the frequency within the sound waves of their voice or by the familiar sound unique to that shepherd, the sheep knew who to follow. They knew the voice of the one whom they trusted.[5]

The Voice of Our Shepherd

Just as shepherds care for and protect their sheep and lead them by the sound of their voice, Jesus does the same for us. He said, "The sheep recognize the voice of the true Shepherd, for he calls his own by name and leads them out, for they belong to him. And when he has brought out all his sheep, he walks ahead of them and they will follow him, for they are familiar with his voice" (John 10:3–4).

Jesus calls us by name and leads us out of whatever "pen" we have been in. He walks ahead of us, leading us with His voice. His voice always aligns with His Word. He speaks in whispers of loving affection, encouragement, and direction. Metaphorically, His voice is the rod used to startle us back toward the flock. Likewise, His voice is the stone we sling at the enemy and take down the dark forces we fight against.

When we speak His Word, His voice goes forth from our mouth and protects us, fights for us, and calms us. Sometimes, He speaks words of correction when we get off course, but never to condemn or shame us; it is always done in love for the purpose of drawing us back to Himself. As our Good Shepherd, Jesus' care for us goes beyond the natural realm. He draws us unto Himself that we will *know* Him and follow in His footsteps.

Listen to His heart: "I alone am the Good Shepherd, and I know those whose hearts are mine, for they recognize me and know me, just as my Father knows my heart and I know my Father's heart" (John 10:14–15). There is so much intimacy described here. He knows whose hearts are His by how He is recognized and known. Our hearts connect with His. We recognize Him when we *know* Him— His essence, His character, the very nature of His being. Because of our time following after His footsteps and listening as He speaks, we know the sound of His voice.

We walk terrain while on earth that can be extremely challenging and sometimes dangerous and painful. The reality Jesus offers us is the same David experienced. Regardless of the terrain, He is good, He is present, and He walks with us. Jesus tenderly cares for us. He is the rod that comforts us, and His Word is the stone we sling to win our battles. His voice goes forth as He calls His sheep, but the question is whether we will respond and fully *embrace and take hold of* Him as our Good Shepherd.

Points to Ponder

- Identify one way that Jesus has recently protected you and what "tool" He used to do so.
- Jesus is always speaking. What do you hear your Good Shepherd saying to you right now?

Prayer of Embrace

Jesus, You are so good, and I am blessed to know that You are my shepherd. Thank You for fiercely protecting me as You watch over me and lead me to safe and bountiful pastures. Help me to recognize when Your rod is leading me away from harm as You punish the enemy on my behalf. Jesus, I know Your voice, so help me to hear and heed Your Word when You speak. Amen.

Chapter 8

Comforting Staff

Even when your path takes me through the valley
of deepest darkness, fear will never conquer me,
for you already have! Your authority is my strength and
my peace. The comfort of your love takes away my fear.
—Psalms 23:4—

Our kind Shepherd, watch over us,
the flock that is your special inheritance.
With your staff, lead your people to pasture.
—Micah 7:14—

As I shared in the previous chapter, the Lord reminded me one morning that He was the Good Shepherd and that He was always with me, regardless of the terrain or the circumstances surrounding me. He also said, *"A shepherd has a staff for a reason,"* and He instructed me to learn what that means. As I researched, it became clear that "staff" is another name by which we can know Jesus.

A staff is one of the tools used in ancient times to shepherd flocks of sheep. The purpose of the staff is multifaceted. If a newborn lamb were somehow separated from its mother, the shepherd could use the curved end to lift and carry it back to its mother. Utilizing the staff to carry the lamb keeps it free from human scent, which would cause it to be rejected. The curved end could also lift a sheep back to safety if it happened upon some precarious cliffs.

Additionally, a shepherd's staff was extremely helpful in guiding the sheep through a new gate or along a dangerous, difficult route. If necessary, the slender stick would be pressed gently against the animal's side, providing pressure and assurance while guiding it to the proper path. Truly, a shepherd's staff is a comforting instrument of protection and care. In addition to all of its purposes for the sheep, the staff was also useful for the shepherd. He could tuck the curved portion under his arm and lean on it when tired and in need of support.

Branch

The Hebrew word for staff is *matte,* and the first meaning listed in the Strong's is branch. In the natural realm of thinking, this may seem unimpressive because a wooden staff would obviously be fashioned from a branch of a tree. But if we allow ourselves to think with our heart and ponder spiritual truths, a new meaning comes to life. Just as a tree's branches extend out from its trunk, Jesus is *the* righteous Branch mentioned in Isaiah 4:2 and Jeremiah 23:5, 33:15. He is the Tree of Life that stood in Eden, from which we all grow. It is His own righteousness that Jesus extends to us, and it is only by fastening ourselves to Him that each believer receives the righteousness He offers.

Tribe

Figuratively, "staff" can mean tribe. A leader's staff identified them with the tribe they led. Based on their role, the leader of each tribe could, in essence, be considered a shepherd over the people within their tribe. In this context, Moses became the shepherd of God's people after encountering His fiery presence and being commissioned to deliver them from Egypt.

When Moses sought to prove his god-given authority to Pharaoh, the Lord directed his attention to the staff in his hand. "Then Moses answered, 'But behold, they will not believe me or listen to my voice, for they will say, "The LORD did not appear to you."' The LORD said to him, 'What is that in your hand?' He said, 'A staff'" (Exodus 4:1–2 ESV). His staff became a symbol of his leadership of the tribe of Israel.

A Rod to Correct, a Scepter to Rule

I find it interesting that the Hebrew word *matte* also means "of a rod," as in a scepter for ruling or a rod for chastising. Both rod and staff speak of the authority to chasten or bring correction. As covered previously, the correction of the rod was never toward the sheep, but rather their predators; the staff, on the other hand, offered gentle, comforting correction for the sheep when needed.

The word "scepter" implies the authority to rule. A staff, then, was also indicative of one's authority. Yahweh established Moses' authority and directed him to use his staff to demonstrate that authority, saying, "Take in your hand this staff, with which you shall do the signs" (Exodus 4:17 ESV). Moses' staff was the evidence of his authority and became the point of contact for the signs, wonders, and miracles that confirmed his authority.

Walking Staff

One last meaning of the Hebrew word *matte* is walking staff. A shepherd could tuck the curved portion of the staff under his arm and lean on it when tired or stick it in the ground when walking to help pull him forward as he ascended hilly terrain. Figuratively, the walking staff is symbolic of a support of life and goes as far as meaning bread.

Bread doesn't seem to fit with the typical meanings for rod and staff, does it? And yet, Jesus Himself told us in John 6:35, "I am the Bread of Life." Metaphorically, a staff in the hand of a shepherd was bread for the sheep in the sense that they were guided to safe pastures in which to feed. And the staff provided bread for the shepherd in the sense that his livelihood was caring for his flock.

In Matthew 13:34, we are told, "Whenever Jesus addressed the crowds, he always spoke in allegories. He never spoke without using parables." It is in the allegories that He draws us closer to Him to gain meaning. This is exactly what He did the morning He reminded me that He is my Good Shepherd and prompted me to learn more. He presented me with a bit of mystery, prodding me to search for deeper understanding.

Learning the full meaning of what a staff was and what it represented and symbolized in ancient times has helped me to embrace this *name* of Jesus. I will likely never refer to Him as "Staff"; however, I can easily take hold of the essence of Him as the "Branch of Righteousness" whom I have been grafted into. Each one of us who has been fastened to the Tree of Life by receiving Jesus now has the ability to produce His fruit of righteousness.

As the head of our tribe, Jesus holds all authority and will correct us. He won't, however, chastise us in the sense of punishment because He took all our punishment upon Himself. Often, what we view as God punishing us is simply the result of our own choices, poor decisions, or alignments with the wrong people or groups. When Jesus offers us correction, it is to guide us onto His path of righteousness. He doesn't rule with an iron rod of harshness. As our tribe leader, He rules over us with a scepter of love. He is kind and gentle and has empowered us to follow His example.

When I think about taking hold of Jesus as my staff, I picture an image of myself hiking up some rough terrain with a walking staff in my right hand. The right hand is a metaphor for authority, and what we hold in our hand is what gives us authority. The authority He has given us is to bring care, guidance, and protection to those around us in our sphere of influence. We are authorized to lovingly lead others higher in the heavenly realm.

As the one in authority over us, Jesus guides us back to safety when we get off track and graciously lifts us out of any pit we fall into. He is the one who steadies us on His ascending path.[1] With our hand holding onto our *Staff,* we can pull on Him each step of the way. He is always right before us, offering support in everyday life as our source of strength.

At times, our path will be smooth like a freshly paved road, allowing enjoyment and peace. Other times, that path will be rough, like a hiking trail covered with gravel and occasional boulders or logs to navigate around. No matter the terrain, walking creates hunger and a need for nourishment, fuel for our journey. As we traverse with our *Staff* in hand, we have *bread* for sustenance as well.

Jesus emphasized the word good that early morning when He called me to know Him as my Good Shepherd. We face many situations and circumstances that are *not* good, but Jesus is always good! He also assures us that He is always with us. No matter what, He is present to help us navigate the path ahead.

Jesus is the branch who is our staff. He is the leader of our tribe, and He has all authority to rule, care for, and lead us. Jesus is the one we lean upon for support during times of weariness. He pulls us forward as we tread the path before us, and He is the Bread of Life that sustains us day by day. We receive the comfort we need by *embracing and taking hold of* Jesus as our Staff.

Points to Ponder

- Which meaning of staff speaks the most to you currently?
- Identify one area of your life that will benefit from applying the reality of Jesus as your comforting staff.

Prayer of Embrace

Jesus, thank You for being my comforting staff, the branch of righteousness that I cling to. Thank You for always leading me back to You when I drift and being my comfort as You protect and correct me. Thank You, Jesus, that You are gentle and kind, and the correction You bring me is not harsh but full of love. Help me to respond quickly to Your leading, knowing I can trust Your authority over my heart and life, even when I don't understand what is going on around me. I am grateful that I can hold onto You as I walk the terrain each day presents, comforted and sustained every step of the way. Amen.

Chapter 9

Curator

There is no great achievement that is not
the result of patient working and waiting.
—Josiah Gilbert Holland—

The leader ... is rarely the brightest person in the group.
Rather they have extraordinary taste, which makes them
more curators than creators. They are appreciators
of talent and nurturers of talent and they have
the ability to recognize valuable ideas.
—Warren G. Bennis—

It can sometimes seem we've been put aside, maybe even forgotten. At those times, it is easy to feel a lack of purpose. Feeling this way isn't limited to a particular age, gender, race, or culture. So often, we put in the work, pursue the dream, and reach for the goal, only to feel like we never achieve or accomplish them. There isn't a formula that works for everyone; however, we can be confident that Jesus holds all the details of our lives in His hands, and we can trust His plan and His timing.

Feeling set aside, forgotten, and unfulfilled are sentiments I have experienced more than I have cared to. It can be depressing when dreams seem out of reach and hopes are deferred. One morning during such a season in my life, the Lord graciously spoke to me. As I sat quietly waiting on Him, a black and white picture of my corner kitchen cabinet came to my mind's eye. Then the picture zoomed in on one of my special mugs sitting on the middle shelf behind the glass pane. I was struck by the awareness that it was functional yet tucked away and unused.

Simultaneously, the Lord began to speak. Among the many words He spoke was the statement, *"I've been curating you."* I had a vague understanding of what it is to curate, but since it isn't in my everyday vocabulary, I paused right then to look up the definition.

Traditionally, to curate is to select and organize items for a collection or exhibition in a museum. In our modern times, this applies to online forums as well, whether the organization of information for research or items for shopping. In relation to arts events and programs, a curator selects the performers and performances that will be featured.[1] As a noun, a curate is a member of the clergy, a minister with pastoral responsibility.[2] In a moment's time, I was flooded with warmth and a sense of security that I didn't realize I needed. The Lord had spoken to my innermost being—to a void deep inside me.

Not only was He reassuring me that He had selected me and set me on the shelf of His storeroom, so to speak, but He was also assuring me that He had been pastoring me. He had been watching over me and keeping me safe within the boundaries of His care. It wasn't that I would never leave the shelf, but rather, He knew the exact time that was right for me to be used. During my waiting, He was also gathering the other "pieces" of the exhibit He had fashioned me for. God is also curating you. He wants you to know Him as your curator so you can trust in His plan to unveil you for His glory.

Our Heavenly Curator

God is our heavenly curator, and Jesus is His most outstanding exhibit. Before He created a thing, God activated a plan of redemption for humanity. He could have orchestrated history to bring the Messiah immediately after Adam fell, yet He chose to wait.

There was a lot of waiting for God's people. Noah waited for decades for the earth to be cleansed while he built the ark. Abraham waited for twenty-five years before his promised son, Isaac, was born. The Israelites waited four centuries before their deliverer led them out of Egypt. David waited on the Lord until his promise to be king became reality. And God's people waited a few millennia for the Messiah to come.

All the while, many tragedies took place, and God's people strayed from Him over and over. As we look back through the Old Testament, it is easy to question why God didn't send Jesus sooner, but He had a specific time set. He had a plan. The lineage of each person, including Mary and Joseph, and the specifics of their lives, were carefully orchestrated to bring a culmination of the fulfillment of multiple prophecies in the birth of Jesus.

Not one person's situation was happenstance, nor was any detail by chance. God was curating the history of each tribe and bringing His plan to fulfillment, regardless of human error. In fact, He knew the will of each person and what they would do in their given situations, and He worked within those parameters. He knew who would love Him and who would reject Him. He knew the ones whose hearts were soft and pliable and those whose hearts were hard and impenetrable. Through it all, He brought forth His plan, in His time.

Manifestation of Salvation

Then salvation manifested! God's masterful curation of bringing His one and only Son into the world finally happened. And He came with spectacular fanfare! First, the heavenly host lit the sky and announced the arrival of Heaven's King to mere shepherds. Second, a royal procession of foreign kings made their way over great distances to bring Him honor and riches, fulfilling more prophecies.

He even curated the final details. Jesus was born to lowly people, and those around Him didn't recognize Him as king, with the exception of Joseph, Mary, Mary's aunt Elizabeth, and the wise men, who had been watching for the sign of His arrival. God kept Jesus from public awareness until it was His time.

One reason for His hiddenness was for protection from the imminent danger of being slaughtered by the threatened King Herod. Another reason was to fulfill more prophecies. By directing Joseph to take Mary and Jesus into Egypt for safety, God also fulfilled His Word spoken through the prophet Hosea: "I summon my Son out of Egypt" (11:1).

When God spoke to Joseph to leave Egypt and return to the land of Israel, He led him to the village of Nazareth in the land of Galilee. This act fulfilled what God spoke hundreds of years prior through Daniel, Isaiah, Jeremiah, and Zechariah: He would bring forth a "Branch." The Hebrew word for branch is *netzer*, which is the root word for Nazareth and Nazarene.[3] Growing up in Nazareth not only fulfilled prophecy, it also kept Jesus tucked away, out of the spotlight, until it was time for His ministry to begin, and it confounded the religious establishment.

Jesus was content to wait for His Father's timing. He had such profound wisdom at the age of twelve that the Jewish teachers who heard Him "were awestruck at His intelligent understanding of all that was being discussed and at His wise answers to their questions"

(Luke 2:47). Many young men at this age might have been filled with selfish ambition and begged to remain in the temple to rise as a star student of an elite teacher. Not Jesus.

In fact, many years later at the marriage in Cana, His words to Mary reveal His contentment to wait for His appointed time: "My hour of unveiling my power has not yet come" (John 2:4). However, because she pulled on His power in faith, He responded. It's as if God the Father, our heavenly curator, allowed the exhibit of His Son to preview earlier than planned because He was so touched by the faith of Mary—this woman whom He highly favored.

Jesus Holds Our Timing and Orchestrates Our Path

As we read the Gospels, we see how Jesus curated His ministry. Each disciple was chosen by Him, knowing their history, their full value, and exactly how they fit into His plan. He didn't disclose His thoughts and plans to just anyone. He was strategic about where, when, and how He traveled. Jesus curated the disciples by teaching, training, and positioning them through everyday experiences and daily life.

After His resurrection, Jesus continued to reveal the Kingdom of Heaven to His disciples, commissioning them to do the same everywhere they went. He provided some insight about what He had prepared them for but told them they must wait for Holy Spirit to seize them with power. They must have felt intense anticipation. How exciting! I can imagine them saying, "Holy Spirit is going to seize us with power!" What imaginations they must've had! Surely it would be even better than when they had been sent out two by two. And I'm sure they were remembering how Jesus told them they would do greater things than He had done.[4] They simply had to wait...but He didn't tell them how long.

Strategically and Individually Curated

Let's think of the museum storeroom, with its many pieces awaiting presentation. Some pieces may require cleaning to accentuate their beauty while preserving their original design. For a curator of an arts event, there is much consideration as to the layout of the vast array of styles and mediums of artwork.

As a former dance mom, I remember learning how much thought and consideration go into curating the performances featured in a yearly dance recital. Some dancers are in multiple dances and have to change costumes and sometimes their hairdos. There is variation in what side of the stage to enter from, and if used, props must be placed strategically.

Give some thought to your life and the fact that you are masterfully designed and fashioned for a purpose. To facilitate that purpose, strategic curating is taking place. Parts of our purpose and commission are refined as we go forward. Other parts need to be placed on the shelf until we experience necessary personal growth and development. Or maybe we are waiting for other "pieces" (people, resources, opportunities) required to help us shine more gloriously.

Whatever the specifics you are waiting on, whatever prophetic words you are contending for, do not lose hope. Instead, let hope arise! If you feel like you have been on the shelf, forgotten and left behind, do not be dismayed. Be encouraged because Jesus has selected you and is curating you. In fact, He tells us that "before we were even born, he gave us our destiny; that we would fulfill the plan of God who always accomplishes every purpose and plan in his heart" (Ephesians 1:11).

As a lover and follower of Jesus, you have been given the same commission He gave His disciples before He ascended. However, both you and I have specifics that others don't, and Jesus knows exactly how He wants those specifics to be utilized and highlighted. He has orchestrated a plan.

Whether we are actively living within the "exhibit" God has specifically fashioned us for or are still in waiting, we can take heart in the final meaning of curate: pastor. Jesus is pastoring each of us. Jesus knows what we need and when. He leads us from one pasture to the next, with perfect timing, while we're in the preparation process.

During this process, we are never forgotten. Jesus never overlooks us. He is carefully, thoughtfully, and intentionally curating us for His unique plan and purpose for our lives. He has implemented a long-range plan for each of us that is often mysterious to us, but never to Him.[5] One last thought: Imagine with me a beautiful vase. It is simple, but elegant. Now imagine its placement in an exhibit. What pieces are surrounding it? Is it positioned high or low? Front and center? To the side or back? Each of us sees a different size, color, shape, and design. The placement of the vase and its surrounding pieces varies widely based on each of our unique imaginations.

Through this exercise, we can see how we tend to have an idea of how things will look. While it is good to imagine and allow ourselves to dream of the possibilities to come, we must keep in mind that Jesus may not bring our preconceived notions to pass. In fact, considering the life stories recorded within the Bible, differing details are likely.

Our ultimate goal is to allow God to position us wherever, however, and whenever He chooses. When it feels like we have been put aside, unnoticed on the shelf of His storeroom, we can shift our heart into trusting our loving curator. He is cultivating His fruit and character within us while we wait. We can hold fast to our prophetic promises and be faithful and obedient until He takes us off the shelf and out of obscurity. If we yield our expectations and keep our hearts open to Him, we are better able to *embrace and take hold of* Jesus as our personal Curator.

Points to Ponder

- Do you sometimes feel forgotten or "put on a shelf"? How has Jesus been curating you during this time?
- In what specific way has Jesus pastored you during your waiting time?
- How does knowing Jesus as your curator shift your heart concerning times of waiting for hopes and dreams to come to pass?

Prayer of Embrace

Jesus, Thank You that in times when I feel put aside, I can rest assured that I am not forgotten. Thank You, Jesus, that You not only place me carefully upon the shelf in Your storeroom, but You are there with me. Help me to be at peace as You heal and restore any fractures within my soul and polish my character in the areas needed. Help me to also be at peace with Your choice as to how and when You bring me off the shelf and into the exhibit You have purposed me for. I trust You, Jesus, as my personal curator. Amen.

Chapter 10

Revelation-Light, More Than Just a Light

There was nothing dark and hidden about Jesus.
He was and is the Light of the world,
and He welcomed the light.
—Samuel Logan Brengle, *Ancient Prophets*—

Don't be fearful about the journey ahead; don't worry about
where you are going or how you are going to get there.
If you believe in the first person of the Trinity, God the
Father, also believe in the second person of the Trinity,
the one who came as the Light of the World, not only to die
for people, but to light the way... This one, Jesus Christ, is
himself the Light and will guide your footsteps along the way.
—Edith Schaeffer, *The Way of Seeing*—

Jesus is the Light of the World. Whenever I heard this
statement growing up, the brilliant light of the sun was what came to
mind. I don't think that's a wrong picture, but because we tend to see
Jesus only through our natural lens, we limit the fullness of knowing
Him as the Light He truly is. The Light of Jesus is so much more.

Each day, the sun peaks over the horizon, chasing darkness away and revealing what already existed, but was hidden by the absence of light. The same is true of Jesus. He is revelation-light, revealing our Heavenly Father and the reality of His Kingdom to those with open hearts. When we open ourselves to Jesus and embrace Him as revelation-light, we gain sight into heavenly matters that we weren't aware of and didn't realize we lacked.

In Acts 9, Saul, the Pharisee of Pharisees, was on a mission. He loved Yahweh with such devout passion that he was pursuing permission to kill every heretic who proclaimed Jesus as Messiah. This was his service to Yahweh. I feel safe to assume that Saul was full of self-assurance that Yahweh was glorified by his fiery determination to eliminate Christians...until he saw the light. A light so incredibly bright and brilliant that Saul was blinded and fell to his knees. This was no ordinary light offered by the sun. This was revelation-light. This was Jesus.

So many of us would have done to Saul what he had been doing to Christians. But not Yahweh. He saw the depth of devotion Saul had for Him. Saul was a lover of the Law, taught under the veil of religion. Jesus came and revealed the truth of who He was, opening Saul's eyes to a reality that had been there all along.

God Is the Source of ALL Revelation-Light

Revelation is simply an act of revealing or making something known, especially an enlightening or astonishing disclosure. Revelation is also an act of revealing or communicating divine truth or something that is revealed by God to humans.[1] Throughout Scripture, we read of humans encountering God and receiving revelation. Basically, God shines His revelation-light to teach or reveal truths or realities that have been present all along, but not realized or embraced.

As creator, God is the source of all revelation-light; in fact, the first recorded creative act of God was Him speaking light into existence. God is the light of Genesis 1:4; after all, the sun and moon didn't exist until Day 4. His glory manifested and sent darkness running. David knew this reality and declared it in Psalm 18:28: "God, all at once you turned on a floodlight for me! You are the revelation-light in my darkness, and in your brightness I can see the path ahead."

Once the sun was spoken into existence, it revealed the land, sea, and vegetation that already existed to sustain the living creatures of Day 5 and the human beings of Day 6. In the same way, God's revelation-light reveals spiritual realities that already exist but have not been seen yet. Everything God created in the physical realm represents a spiritual reality.

Jesus—*The* Revelation-Light

The spiritual reality of God being revelation-light was manifested in the physical person of Jesus. Luke recorded the prophetic utterance of Simeon, a lover of God, who was present when Mary and Joseph brought Jesus into the temple shortly after his birth: "With my own eyes I have seen your Word, the Savior you sent into the world. He will be glory for your people Israel, and the Revelation-Light for all people everywhere!" (Luke 2:31–32). Simeon knew the prophecies of Isaiah and was blessed to not only see but literally hold the glorious revelation-light of God.[2]

Matthew 4:16 quotes Isaiah 9:2: "You who spend your days shrouded in darkness can now say, 'We have seen a brilliant Light.'" What is especially fascinating about this Scripture is that, according to rabbinical literature, light is a common name for Messiah, speaking both of Jesus and His revelatory teachings. Equally fascinating is the fact that the Aramaic word for Galilee means "revelation of God,"[3] so Jesus grew up and ministered in the land of the "revelation of God."

Once Jesus began His ministry, He spoke to reveal the Kingdom of Heaven and His Father, the source of light. He shed light on the Torah, revealing meaning to those with ears to hear. John testified of Jesus, saying, "A fountain of life was in him, for his life is light for all humanity. And this Light never fails to shine through darkness—Light that darkness could not overcome!" (John 1:4–5). He also testified of John the Baptist's mission in verses 7 and 9, declaring, "For he came as a witness, to point the way to the Light of Life, and to help everyone believe ... For the perfect Light of Truth was coming into the world and shine upon everyone."

Jesus added to the proclamation in John 8:12: "I am light to the world, and those who embrace me will experience life-giving light, and they will never walk in darkness." How can we never walk in darkness when it's a part of each twenty-four-hour cycle? This statement couldn't be accurate if He were speaking of the physical realm. However, if we join His way of thinking, we understand Jesus was speaking of the reality that many humans walk in spiritual darkness with their natural eyes wide open in the full light of day. His words in John 12:46 make this reality clearer: "I have come as a light to shine in *this dark world* so that all who trust in me will no longer wander in darkness" (emphasis added).

The Purpose of Revelation-Light

Reveal the Father

There are many purposes for revelation-light, many more than I will cover, but the first I'd like to point out is to reveal. As the revelation-light, Jesus' purpose was to reveal the Father: "For when you look at me you are seeing the One who sent me" (John 12:45). The Father had always been present, but not seen. Jesus not only revealed the Father, but also the word of the Father as He taught in the temple and on the hillside.

Life-Giving Light

Jesus made it plain in John 8:12, mentioned above, that embracing Him brings the experience of life-giving light. Think of Saul of Tarsus. Even though he was among the religious elite of all religious leaders and knew the Torah, he was not experiencing life-giving light. He lived in and from darkness, separated from God. He was alive in his natural body but spiritually dead and bringing death to others. He was one hundred percent against Jesus, loathing everyone who bore the name Christian. It was Saul's blinding encounter with revelation-light that opened his eyes and his heart to the reality that he had been living in spiritual darkness, blinded to the truth.

Salvation and Protection

Long before Jesus came in an earthen vessel to reveal the Father, David knew revelation-light. He proclaimed in Psalm 27:1, "YAHWEH is my revelation-light and the source of my salvation. I fear no one! I'll never turn back and run, for you, YAHWEH, surround and protect me." David received revelation through his intimacy with God that made him confident of his salvation. Yet he experienced many trials. So revelation-light doesn't keep trials from coming but surrounds and protects us in the midst of them.

Training

David prayed in Psalm 25:9, "Keep showing the humble your path, and lead them into the best decision. Bring revelation-light that trains them in the truth." He prayed this for others because he experienced it himself and knew the value of being trained by revelation-light. John testified of how Jesus trained him and the other disciples: "Moses gave us the Law, but Jesus, the Anointed One, unveils truth wrapped in tender mercy. ... Now that He has come to us, He has unfolded the full explanation of who God truly is!" (John 1:17–18).

As we humble ourselves before God and yield to His leading, revelation-light trains us in truth and knowing God.

Guide

A flashlight is often used when walking in the dark. We live in a dark world, and we need a light to guide us. Psalm 119:105 tells us that "truth's shining light guides me in my choices and decisions; the revelation of your Word makes my pathway clear." Jesus is that "Word." When we don't know what to do or which way to go, literally or metaphorically, we can focus on Jesus, and He will shed light on our situations and guide us in our decisions.

Correction

Some of us cringe when we hear the word correction, especially when it comes to spiritual correction. This is probably due to times when well-meaning (or maybe not-so-well-meaning) leaders have used Scripture to manipulate, control, or shame us into better behavior. That type of correction is pharisaical and not like Jesus; He didn't come to condemn but to rescue us from condemnation.[4]

There are times we need the guidance of others to better live out Scripture, but truly, God's design is that we live in such intimacy with Him that we are "flooded with His Revelation-Light" and respond to Him when He highlights sin, false beliefs, or wrong mindsets that aren't in alignment with His Word (Ephesians 5:8). Paul taught this in Ephesians 5:13: "Whatever the revelation-light exposes, it will also correct, and everything that reveals truth is light to the soul."

We can be at rest and know that if our hearts are open to revelation-light, Jesus will reveal the areas of our lives still in need of transformation. As we gladly receive His correction, we continue the process of becoming like Him. The key is to keep our hearts tender before the

Lord and heed the warning in Luke 11:34–35: "When your heart is hard and closed, the light cannot penetrate and darkness takes its place. ... Watch out that you do not mistake your opinions for revelation-light!"

There are a couple of ways I commonly receive correction. One is through His Word, whether by reading it or hearing someone preach or teach it. An undeniable awareness comes and highlights a specific situation to which the truth presented needs to be applied. A second way is by the whisper of His voice as Holy Spirit speaks to my spirit. For example, once I was ruminating over a difficult situation and imagining what I would say if given the opportunity, and I heard, *"That is manipulation."* It "sounded" like my own thoughts, but it was the loving voice of my Father. I quickly repented and asked Him to heal that area in my heart that caused me to think in such a way. There have been times He has spoken quite firmly, but even in those moments, I felt loved, comforted, and empowered to make the necessary change. When the Lord corrects, He doesn't condemn or shame.

Transformation

Revelation-light also releases power for transformation. As we are consumed with Jesus, His light fills us and shines through us. He transforms our dull earthen vessels into radiant vessels of glory. Once again, we gain insight through David's intimate relationship with Yahweh in Psalm 19:8: "YAHWEH's teachings are right and make us joyful; his precepts are so pure! YAHWEH's commands challenge us to keep close to his heart! The revelation-light of his Word makes my spirit shine radiant."

As a young shepherd boy, David would've been considered lowly and insignificant, but he didn't allow his status to determine his worth. David yielded to Yahweh's teachings and shone radiantly. God used his time in the fields with the sheep to transform his heart into that of a king.

Saul was transformed when he was confronted by Jesus on the road to Damascus. He went from being a pompous Pharisee, furiously persecuting the church, to Paul, the humble bondservant of Christ, whose "power increased greatly as he became more and more proficient in proving that Jesus was the anointed Messiah" (Acts 9:22). He opened his heart and allowed revelation-light to flood in and shine through him!

Commissioning

Before ascending and sending Holy Spirit, Jesus commissioned all believers to go forth and preach the good news. The good news is that we have the option to leave the darkness and enter light because we are no longer condemned because of Jesus' finished work on the cross. Once transformed, Paul spent his life preaching the gospel as commissioned by Jesus:

> Get up and stand to your feet, for I have appeared to you to reveal your destiny and to commission you as my assistant. You will be a witness to what you have seen and to the things I will reveal whenever I appear to you. ... And you will open their eyes to their true condition, so that they may turn from darkness to the Light and from the power of Satan to the power of God. By placing their faith in me they will receive the total forgiveness of sins and be made holy, taking hold of the inheritance that I give to my children!

> — Acts 26:16, 18

That which Paul experienced, he sought to impart to others. He prayed for the Ephesian church, and ultimately each of us, that "the light of God will illuminate the eyes of your imagination, flooding you with light, until you experience the full revelation of the hope of his calling—that is, the wealth of God's glorious inheritances that he finds in us, his holy ones!" (Ephesians 1:18).

He was straightforward as he called people higher, telling them plainly, "Once your life was full of sin's darkness, but now you have the very light of our Lord shining through you because of your union with him. Your mission is to live as children flooded with his revelation-light!" (Ephesians 5:8).

The Hebrew and Greek words used for revelation-light in the Scriptures I've referenced all have very similar meanings. It means to be or make luminous, to give light, set on fire, shine. It also means to glisten and denotes the burner of a lamp and light. It is bright and full of light. And it also means to make manifest and fire. This is Jesus. He is the luminous one who manifests Himself, revealing His way and the essence of who He is. He is full of light and illuminates the dark areas of our understanding. He is the fire that shines bright and the burner that lights our lamp, setting us on fire for Him. Jesus is *the* light, but not just any light...revelation-light.

As our revelation-light, Jesus reveals the Kingdom of Heaven and the deeper meaning hidden in the Word of God. He is life-giving light, drawing mankind out of death's darkness. He is our salvation and protection, offering us deliverance, welfare, prosperity, and liberty. As we walk upon His path for our life, He trains us in truth and guides us in our choices and situations, lovingly correcting us along the way. By embracing and yielding to revelation-light, we are transformed from the inside out. We carry His light within us and are commissioned to reveal Jesus to the people we encounter each day.

When Saul encountered Jesus as a brilliant light, it wasn't his first experience of being blind. His encounter revealed the fact that he had been blind to *knowing* Yahweh, even though he had physical sight and knew the Torah. Unfortunately, there are many believers in the same predicament as Saul, thinking life in Christ is about knowing lots of Scripture and following rules. For some, this includes pointing out where others are wrong. Let's pray they experience revelation-light and that the scales are removed from their eyes, allowing them to see Jesus and the Word in a new way, just as Saul did.

What I hope you gain from this chapter is a new perspective of Jesus' declaration that He is light to the world.[5] I also hope you develop an eagerness to heed His statement in Luke 8:17–18:

> Because this revelation lamp now shines within you, nothing will be hidden from you—it will all be revealed. Every secret of the kingdom will be unveiled and out in the open, made known by the revelation-light. So pay careful attention to your hearts as you listen to my teaching, for to those who have open hearts, even more revelation will be given to them until it overflows. And for those who do not listen with open hearts, what little light they imagine themselves to have will be taken away.

Jesus is more than just a light—He is the light of life. He is ever shining to reveal Himself, the Father, and the reality of Heaven's Kingdom. If His light dwells within us and our hearts are open and seeking Him, He is faithful to release to us revelation regarding heavenly matters.

His light releases life and provides salvation and protection, training and guidance, and correction and transformation. And, by His light, He commissions us to be His light to others. All of this and more is available to us as we *embrace and take hold of* Jesus as Revelation-Light.

Points to Ponder

- From the purposes of God's revelation-light listed in this chapter, which one impacted you the most? How so?
- What situation in your life would benefit most from revelation-light?
- Take a moment, open your heart, and see yourself embracing revelation-light. Ask Him to shine upon the situation. What understanding or strategy did you receive?

Prayer of Embrace

Jesus, I open my heart to You and ask that You remove any hindering scales from my eyes, anything that hinders me from seeing You and that which You desire to reveal to me. Open my spirit eyes to Your Kingdom realm. Unveil those things that are right in front of me but not yet seen. Thank You, Jesus, that You are faithful to bring illumination to my understanding and fire to light my lamp so I may burn for You. May I be filled with passion and zeal for you, like David and Paul, as I embrace revelation-light within my being and upon my path. Amen.

Chapter 11

Rebel, Revolutionary, or Both?

Like the early Christians, we must move into
a sometime hostile world armed with the revolutionary
gospel of Jesus Christ. With this powerful gospel
we shall boldly challenge the status quo.
—Martin Luther—

Revolution was and is in each step and breath
of those who dare follow this man called Jesus.
Revolution comes about only when there is at least one
person willing to take a stand for God and say
"the present system" is wrong and thus will not accomplish
the purposes of God. All of God's purposes center on
His glory and meeting the needs of people.
Jesus was the ultimate revolutionary.
—Kip McKean,
Revolution Through Restoration—

IN THE LATE '90S, I PURCHASED A WITNESS WEAR T-SHIRT THAT had a picture of Jesus on the cross and a banner that stated, "Rebel With A Cause." I am inclined to think it was designed in reference to the 1950s movie, *Rebel Without A Cause*. This movie featured a troubled teen rebelling against societal norms and values that seemed hollow and pointless. The message resonated with people, and James Dean, who was a leading character, became a teenage heartthrob and role model.

Some may gasp at the thought of calling Jesus a rebel because of the negative connotation attached to that word. However, there are many ideologies and mindsets that we should rebel against. If Jesus was a rebel, what did He rebel against? Since rebellion is a sin, how could He have anything to do with it? Was He a revolutionary who came to bring reformation? Let's explore these questions and see if Jesus was a rebel, revolutionary, or both.

Not All Rebellion Is Wrong

I remember a conversation I had as a youth pastor with someone about teens and rebellion, and what this person said bothered me. I responded to one of their statements, saying, "I think I would rebel against that too." The fact of the matter is, I knew what was going on, and that teen was right to reject what was being imposed. Sometimes, that which is labeled as rebellious isn't rebellious at all. True rebellion is disobeying God's instructions.

God's set of divine instructions was given to Moses and became the Old Testament Law. From that time forward, God chose prophets, who were His voice and upheld the Law. To disobey God's prophet was the same as disobeying God. In 1 Samuel, King Saul ignored the instructions given to him by the prophet Samuel. He was to wait for Samuel to come and offer sacrifices to God on his behalf. King Saul got impatient and, instead of waiting, he offered the sacrifices himself. When Samuel arrived and discovered King Saul's disobedience, he said, "Rebellion is like the sin of divination, and arrogance like the evil of idolatry" (1 Samuel 15:23 NIV). It seems King Saul thought it was only about performing the ritual.

Centuries later, the priesthood was plagued with the same misunderstanding and became more like a lifeless machine than a ministry of reconciliation for the people. They followed God's Law but not God's heart. It is with this frame of thinking that I propose Jesus was a rebel because during His time on earth, He rebelled against the traditions of men—the religious system—and followed God's heart.

What Jesus Rebelled Against

A person is often considered a rebel if they rise in opposition against leaders or an established system, whether it be a government or an organization. To rebel against God, His Word, and His ways is not good; it's the same as practicing divination, positioning yourself as God. However, it is acceptable to rebel against a demand to submit to a system or any type of leadership that exalts a person, titles, or positions above God. It is also okay to rebel against the requirement to perform good works to earn favor and any demands that lead you into sin. The key to our obedience is to keep our hearts set on following Jesus' example.

Keep in mind, though, that Jesus didn't rebel against the government of earth, and Paul, inspired by the Holy Spirit, wrote specifically about obeying civil authorities in Romans 13. We must be careful to honor our governmental authorities while keeping God's Word as our final authority.

Jesus' example was to obey the Father in all things, submitting to Him as the ultimate authority. He was on a mission to revolutionize people's understanding of God's Kingdom. He may have been a rebel in the eyes of the religious leaders, but He was a rebel in the most positive sense possible.

Who Is Jesus to You?

The following is a scriptural list of things Jesus rebelled against.

Traps of the Enemy

Starting in the wilderness with Satan and continuing with the religious leaders, Jesus rebelled against the traps of the enemy time and time again until His death. Jesus overcame those snares and wiles by speaking the Word of God and living from the reality of His Kingdom.

Religious Systems and Rituals

Just like His forerunner, John the Baptist, Jesus rebelled against the religious system and its rituals that taught people to follow hundreds of laws but neglected to teach them about God's desire for relationship and mercy.

Pomp and Pretense

The Pharisees and other religious leaders liked to be seen and heard in their devotion. Jesus warned in Matthew 6:5, "Whenever you pray, be sincere and not like the pretenders who love the attention they receive while praying before others in the meetings and on the street corners." He rebelled against pomp and pretense by regularly sneaking away to a secluded place to commune with His Father.

Religious Pride

Jesus rebelled against religious pride by dining with Matthew and many other tax collectors and outcasts of society, causing the Pharisees to be indignant and complain. He spoke directly to them, instructing them to "go and study the meaning of the verse: I want you to show mercy, not just offer me a sacrifice. For I have come to invite the outcasts of society and sinners, not those who think they are already on the right path" (Matthew 9:13).

Sabbath Rules

Matthew 12:1–12 holds two of many examples of Jesus rebelling against unnecessary Sabbath rules. He allowed His disciples to harvest grain from the fields, and He healed a man's paralyzed hand. In between these two events, in verse 8, Jesus declared to the accusing Pharisees that "the Son of Man exercises his lordship over the Sabbath."

They thought the Sabbath was all about rules, but they lacked the understanding that true Sabbath rest is mercy. It is humans living in right relationship with God by faith and God meeting the needs of those who rest in Him.

Demands for a Sign

Jesus rebelled against the demands for a sign.[1] No amount of miracles would convince the unbelieving Jewish scholars and Pharisees that Jesus was the Messiah. Jesus was straightforward when He replied to their demand in Matthew 12:39: "Only evil people who are unfaithful to God would demand a sign." And again in 16:4, He said, "A wicked and wayward generation always asks for signs."

Traditions and Rituals

In Matthew 15:2, the Pharisees and religious leaders asked Jesus, "Why do your disciples ignore the traditions of our elders?" Jesus answered them in 15:3: "And why do you ignore the commandment of God because of your traditions?" Jesus rebelled against heeding traditions over the commands of God.

Imposed and Illegitimate Authority

Those fixated on power are threatened by those who walk in Yahweh's authority. This applies to the leading priests and Jewish elders of Jesus' day and the religious leaders of our day. Matthew 21:23–27 gives an account of these ungodly leaders questioning Jesus' authority to do miracles and teach in the temple courts. Jesus rebelled against their imposed authority, refusing to submit to it. He knew who He was and asserted His God-ordained authority by asking them a question in return. He told them He would answer them after they answered Him. They couldn't.

Hypocrisy

Matthew 23 is full of woes for the religious scholars and Pharisees. These judgments were a direct result of their hypocrisy. Before He proclaimed the woes, Jesus warned His disciples and the crowd to listen and follow what the religious leaders teach, but not do what they do because they "tell you to do one thing and do another" (v. 3). Jesus was true to His word and lived what He preached—He was a rebel against hypocrisy.

Selfishness and Violence

In Matthew 26, Jesus rebelled against selfishness when He yielded to suffering in the garden. He also rebelled against violence by peacefully yielding to arrest and ordering His disciple to put away the dagger used to slash off the ear of the high priest's servant.

And More

Jesus rebelled against darkness by shining the light. He rebelled against the world's system of leadership by being a servant leader, even going to the extreme of humbly washing His disciples' dirty feet.

When Antipas requested a miracle, Jesus refused, rebelling against the pressure to perform for man's approval. Jesus could have spoken in defense of Himself when He was on trial, but instead, He rebelled against self-preservation and laid His life down on the cross. Nothing could cause Him to abort His mission of redeeming His beloved people.

After taking our sin upon Himself, Jesus rebelled against sin's power by nailing it to the cross. It may have seemed that death won when Jesus hung upon the cross and gave up His life, but Jesus rebelled against death by rising from the grave three days later in triumphant victory!

Jesus, the Revolutionary

If evil and injustice are being rebelled against, a rebel could better be considered a revolutionary. In terms of the religious and worldly systems, Jesus was a rebel. Anne Douglas Sedgwick said it well, "Rebels are the people who refuse the seen for the unseen."[2] That is how Jesus lived while on earth. He refused the seen, the natural realm limitations, because He lived from the unseen. While He rebelled against the religious system and refused to submit to the Pharisees and other religious leaders, He did not live in rebellion.

Rebellion is considered opposition to one in authority or an open and armed resistance to an established government.[3] Jesus didn't do either of those. He lived in total surrender and union with the one true authority, Yahweh, His Father. And not once did He take up arms to overthrow the governance of Rome, even though the Jewish people thought Messiah's mission was to do just that.

We are to live like Jesus, in total surrender and union with the Father. We are to be in this world, but not of it. In terms of His Kingdom, Jesus was a revolutionary. He dramatically changed the way mankind related to God. A revolutionary brings about a revolution, causes a complete or radical change in an organization or in the way people think, and brings a shift in paradigms.[4] That's what Jesus did!

By embracing Jesus as a rebel against religion, we in turn embrace Him as the revolutionary who brought the Kingdom of Heaven to earth. As a revolutionary, He demonstrated God's love through authoritative power *and* tender compassion. He revolutionized the set way of thinking by turning traditional understanding upside down. Jesus brought about a complete change in many established mindsets. Here are a few:

- Salvation is not by works—it is only by grace and through childlike faith.
- There is no hate in the Kingdom of God—only love.
- We are not called to retaliation—only forgiveness and blessing.
- We do not live in bondage to the Law—we live by the impulses of Holy Spirit.

The message written on the back of the t-shirt I mentioned earlier reads, *"Jesus went against religion to bring a relationship with God, against sin to bring forgiveness, and His body was placed against the cross to bring salvation."* Truly, He was a Rebel With a Cause.

Aristotle once said, "Those who excel in virtue have the best right of all to rebel, but then they are of all men the least inclined to do so."[5] This must not be true of those who have been given the authority to be children of God. Our mission is to live in union with Him, spend time in His presence, exude His very essence, and partner with Him to revolutionize the world around us. We must *take hold of* Jesus as a rebel against the religious and worldly systems, and simultaneously *embrace* Him as a Revolutionary.

Points to Ponder

- What stirs within you as you think of Jesus as a rebel?
- Name one area of your life in which there is a need to righteously rebel. Ask Holy Spirit what He has for you in that area instead. What did He say?
- As the most profound revolutionary to have ever walked the earth, in what way can you identify yourself with Jesus? In what way are you being stirred to become more like Him?

Prayer of Embrace

Jesus, I want to live surrendered to the Father, just as You demonstrated. Anoint me with holy discernment to know what is of You and what to rebel against. I do not desire to go through motions that lack intimacy. I want to live and move by the impulses of Your Holy Spirit. Help me be like You and rebel against the religious system that lacks love and transformational power. Help me instead to embrace Your love and transformational power to revolutionize my life and the lives of those in my sphere of influence. Amen.

Chapter 12

Resurrection

Death is the ultimate weapon of the tyrant; resurrection does
not make a covenant with death, it overthrows it.
—N.T. Wright,
The Resurrection of the Son of God—

There is this difference between the growth of some human
beings and that of others: in the one case it is a continuous
dying, in the other a continuous resurrection.
—George MacDonald—

So live in the light of the resurrection and renewal
of this world, and of yourself, in a glorious,
never-ending, joyful dance of grace.
—Timothy J. Keller, *King's Cross*—

"I am the Resurrection." These are the words of Jesus in
John 11:25. He made this declaration after Martha acknowledged
that her brother Lazarus would rise on the day of resurrection with
everyone else. Jesus was telling her that she didn't have to wait until

then and said, "Anyone who clings to me in faith, even though he dies, will live forever. And the one who lives by believing in me will never die" (John 11:25–26).

As Christians, we believe Jesus' words, His promise that even though our physical bodies die, our spirits will live forever in God's presence. However, have we pondered what He meant by His last statement to Martha—that those who live by believing in Him will never die? He had to be speaking of another reality, because if He were speaking of our physical body, then we would never attend funerals for Christians. Let's explore the reality of Jesus as *the* Resurrection.

The Grip of Death

Death not only affects our physical body, which will eventually die, but also our spiritual, mental, and emotional well-being. For those who are in Christ, death has lost its grip. But unfortunately, many still live under the dominion of death. By embracing Jesus as the Resurrection, we are empowered to identify and rid our hearts and souls of death's power.

Physically, we experience death when our vital organs stop working. Likewise, death comes to our soul when it is overwhelmed by substances invisible to the natural eye but very real in the spirit realm. Unforgiveness brings death to relationships. Shame brings death to confidence. Religious duty brings death to sincere devotion. Foolishness brings death to wisdom. The fear of man brings death to courage. These toxins poison our souls, creating dis-ease and an inability to function as designed. In these ways and many more, death affects us while we live.

"A thief has only one thing in mind—he wants to steal, slaughter, and destroy. But I have come to give you everything in abundance, more than you expect—life in its fullness until you overflow!" (John 10:10). The thief, Satan, is behind the death and destruction we experience.

Part of Jesus' mission was to teach us how to experience an over-flowing life, full of abundance, while we live on earth. Paul spoke of the "realm of death" as our former state, when we were held in sin's grasp, but declared that those in Christ "have been resurrected out of that "realm of death" never to return, for we are forever alive and forgiven of all our sins" (Colossian 2:13).

More Than One Meaning

Resurrection is well known as the event of Jesus rising from the dead, but it also means resurgence or revival. So we see that the reality of resurrection goes further than bringing someone back to life after their body dies; it includes rising into life and activity, having renewed attention or interest, and restoration of validity.[1] *Anastasis,* the Greek word for resurrection, encompasses the concept of experiencing a moral recovery of spiritual truth.

Resurrection Life destroys death, not only when we are raised to Heaven after we die but also now while we live on earth. As Resurrection Life, Jesus holds the power to re-create and give life instead of death. The moment we are born again, we receive resurrection life that ensures we will abide in God's presence for eternity, but it takes embracing Him as the Resurrection in every aspect of our lives to ensure we will experience the fullness of His resurrection life and power while we remain on earth.

We go from glory to glory as we partner with Resurrection Life.[2] As Holy Spirit highlights areas in our souls needing resurrection, we are transformed into the likeness of Jesus by yielding to His Life *in* us instead of the death surrounding us.

To accept salvation means that we accept the spiritual truth that we were crucified with Christ. The penalty He suffered was on our behalf. Spiritually, you and I hung on the cross with Him: "For you were included in the death of Christ and have died with him" (Colossians 2:20). To accept the life Jesus purchased for us, we must also accept death to our old nature.

Resurrected with Jesus

To live in an embrace with Jesus, the Resurrection, we must also accept the reality of Colossians 3:1 and 3, which states, "Christ's resurrection is your resurrection too. This is why we are to yearn for all that is above, for that's where Christ sits enthroned at the place of all power, honor, and authority! Your crucifixion with Christ has severed the tie to this life, and now your true life is hidden away in God in Christ."

His death was our death, and His resurrection was our resurrection! We aren't just a new person; we are a new species. We are now dust and deity mixed together, just like Jesus. We don't have to accept earthly realities as our truth. With Jesus in us, our spiritual reality is that we have already overcome. Regardless of the magnitude of the challenges we face, we can be like Jesus and fix our gaze on the joy set before us,[3] keeping in mind that the same Spirit that raised Christ from the dead now lives in us—His resurrection life and power are *in* us by Holy Spirit.[4]

Let's revisit Jesus' statement to Martha in John 11:26: "The one who lives by believing in me will never die." To live by believing in Jesus isn't simply believing He is real and that He is God. It is to believe and live according to what He says, above all else. By doing so, we will not engage with death in our mind, soul, or heart while we remain on earth. We can face troubles, pressure, grief, persecution, and so on, by the power of His life in us. We will never die because we will go from living in His abundant life here on earth to eternal life when our earthen vessel is laid to rest. Lazarus was a demonstration of what can happen when we live by believing in Him above our circumstances. Dead things come to life.

Negative mindsets are another aspect of our mortal life that Jesus desires to impact with Resurrection Life. The way we think often brings death. If I believe no one likes me, I will have a hard time connecting with people, regardless of their efforts, because I am partnering with death in my relationships. Similarly, if I hold the belief that nothing ever goes well for me, I will likely experience death in multiple situations. If I believe I can't do something, that belief brings death to opportunities, successes, and forward movement. There is no life in these mindsets.

Living from Resurrection

There are a myriad of ways death can affect us, even without our realizing it. I mentioned a few already, but consider these as well:

- Despair and negativity bring death to hope.
- Criticism brings death to enjoyment.
- Judging others brings death to friendliness and the ability to accept their uniqueness.
- Self-centeredness brings death to community.
- Lying and deceit bring death to trust, and unbelief and doubt bring death to faith.

Holy Spirit knows each of us and what area(s) of our lives needs resurrection. We simply ask, and He reveals. When He reveals an alignment with death in a specific area, we repent for partnering with it and accept and release Resurrection Life in its place. With your mouth, speak the reality of what Jesus says about you and the situation.

Since we are seated with Jesus in heavenly places, we live *from* Heaven *toward* earth, resurrected from the things that bring death.[5] To believe we can embrace Resurrection Life, regardless of our circumstances, isn't denial; it is living from a spiritual reality while living in the physical realm.

This makes me think of Paul's words in Philippians 3:10–13:

>  And I continually long to know the wonders of Jesus and to experience the overflowing power of his resurrection working in me. I will be one with him in his sufferings and become like him in his death. Only then will I be able to experience complete oneness with him in his resurrection from the realm of death. I admit that I haven't yet acquired the absolute fullness that I'm pursuing, but I run with passion into his abundance so that I may reach the purpose for which Christ Jesus laid hold of me to make me his own. I don't depend on my own strength to accomplish this; however, I do have one compelling focus: I forget all of the past as I fasten my heart to the future instead.

May we, like Paul, continually long to experience the overflowing power of resurrection. We may not acquire its fullness while living in our mortal bodies, but we can certainly pursue it and experience it in increasing measures. I believe Jesus would ask each of us the same question He asked Martha before demonstrating His power as *the* Resurrection: "Do you believe this?" (John 11:26).

The question wasn't whether she believed in resurrection or if she was certain her brother would live forever. Martha had already attested that she did. The question was more about whether she believed that a person could live a life free of death by believing in Him. Did she believe that *He* was *the Resurrection* that made Spirit-empowered living possible?

Jesus resurrecting people from the dead isn't the same as Jesus *being* the Resurrection. You are empowered to overthrow death because

Who Is Jesus to You?

Christ lives in you. Believe it. Believe Him. Experience His power and take back what death has stolen as you *embrace and take hold of* Jesus as *the* Resurrection.

Points to Ponder

- How does embracing Jesus as Resurrection Life shift your mindset about never dying?
- Is there an area in your life that needs to embrace resurrection? What is it?
- In the area you identified above, search for a Scripture that reveals what Jesus wants you to experience instead.

Prayer of Embrace

Jesus, I acknowledge You as the Resurrection. You conquered death, and You are eternal life. I believe that I will live forever with you after my body dies. I also believe that I can live free from things that bring death while here on earth, because You are the Resurrection. Things that trouble me cannot bring death to me because I am in You, and You are in me. Thank You, Holy Spirit, for revealing mindsets and alignments that have allowed death in my life, and thank You for empowering me to break agreement with death and instead embrace You as Resurrection. Amen.

Chapter 13

Breath of Heaven

The Spirit of God has made me;
the breath of the Almighty gives me life.
—Job 33:4 NIV—

Lord Yahweh says to you: "I am now going
to breathe into you, and you will live again! ...
And you will know that I am Yahweh."
—Ezekiel 37:5–6—

I REMEMBER A TIME WHEN I WAS IN THE THIRD OR FOURTH grade. My dad and I had gone on a bike ride and passed by my school along the way. I wanted to show him how I could hang by my knees from a pull-up bar on the playground, swing back and forth several times, and flip to my feet. I was doing good, swinging higher and higher, upside down, freaking my dad out. I reassured him I was fine, only to release the bar and land flat on the ground.

I thought I was going to die; the air in my lungs had been completely knocked out by the force, and I lay there gasping. My dad rushed to my side, and after panicking a bit himself, he began breathing deeply, coaching me to do the same. I don't remember how long I lay there refilling my lungs, but I will never forget the feeling of not being able to breathe freely.

Life can leave us feeling exasperated, not knowing what to do or say. Sometimes it can feel like the wind has been knocked out of our lungs, and even though we're breathing, it seems we're not. When emotional chaos is swirling, remaining grounded can be difficult. In those moments, it helps to focus on what we know to be true and not allow the temporal situation to convince us otherwise. When the atmosphere around us is disrupted, and we feel like we are left gasping for air, literally or metaphorically, we can focus on Jesus and receive fresh breath from Heaven.

Sustaining Breath

After sculpting Adam from the dust of the earth, God breathed into his nostrils and filled his lungs with His Spirit wind. Adam became a living soul when he received God's breath. Every other living creature God made during the days of creation received the oxygen necessary when God spoke them into existence, but with Adam, God got close and breathed into his nostrils. (Isn't it interesting that we administer mouth-to-mouth resuscitation to provide the breath of life to those in need?)

Air is one of the key elements necessary to sustain the life of every human. This fact is another natural realm reality that mirrors the truth of the spirit realm. God is Spirit, and everything that exists came from Him. So it makes sense that all things originate in the spirit and then manifest in the natural. It stands to reason, then, that if we need air to exist in the natural realm, we need "air" to exist in the spirit. As soon as a baby is born, it must begin breathing to live. Likewise, we receive "air" from Holy Spirit when we accept Jesus, and our spirit is "born again."

Jesus spoke of an eternal truth when He told Nicodemus: "Unless you are born of water and the Spirit, you will never enter God's Kingdom. For the natural realm only gives birth to things that are natural, but the spiritual realm gives birth to supernatural life! You shouldn't be amazed by my statement, 'You all must be born from above!'" (John 3:6–8).

As humans, each of us is born of water. We are cradled in water within our mother's womb, and when her "water breaks," we enter the world and our family. Likewise, receiving eternal life births us into the family of God. Our natural body needs the physical element of oxygen to function, and our spirit needs the breath of God to live and function in the spirit realm. Without it, we are not truly alive.

Jesus Is Our Breath

There are two mentions of God giving us His breath in Scripture. The first is Genesis 2:7, when He blew the breath of life into Adam's nostrils. The second is when Jesus appeared to the disciples after His resurrection: "Then, taking a deep breath, he blew on them and said, 'Receive the Holy Spirit'" (John 20:22). Jesus is the manifested Spirit of God—He is the breath of God.

Just as He blew upon His disciples that day, He continues to blow upon us. However, we must heed the same instruction He gave them: *receive.* We must receive His breath, His Spirit, as He blows upon us.

It's possible to go about our day, facing situations and circumstances of all kinds in our own strength and based on physical realm realities, or we can receive His breath that fills and sustains us. The difference can be so subtle, but the results are often dramatically different.

When Jesus appeared to His disciples that day, they were experiencing great fear. There was a lot of chaos swirling around them due to Jesus' resurrection, and they feared retaliation from the Jewish leaders. Their future lives were uncertain. Everything they had hoped for seemed lost. Their lifestyle of following the Messiah was now blatantly challenged. Things had not gone as they expected; the depth of their confusion must've been intense.

When we speak, our breath travels over our vocal cords, creating vibrations that turn to sound that forms our words. As Jesus stood before His disciples for the first time since His resurrection, He released His breath and spoke the words, "Peace to you!" (John 20:19). At a time when it seemed impossible, Jesus released peace. After showing His wounds to His fearful disciples, He released peace a second time. And then He sent them out to preach the forgiveness of sins.[1] His plan for them was not to hunker down and hide from the threats at hand, but to go and do the work of the Kingdom, bringing Heaven to earth. How? By receiving His breath, which is His Spirit.

Fresh Breath from Heaven

Just like having the air knocked out of our lungs physically, we can experience a similar phenomenon during trials. It can feel like we're suffocating. I remember a time of massive confusion when I was feeling overwhelmed and unsure of a solution. I sensed a subtle prompting from Holy Spirit to begin breathing deeply, slowly, and rhythmically. It was as if He was coaching me like my dad did so long ago when I lay below that pull-up bar.

With my eyes closed, I breathed Him in. In my mind's eye, I envisioned Him flowing in through my nose while I released stress and anxiety with each breath out of my mouth. In a matter of two to three minutes, the situation de-escalated, and the atmosphere shifted. As I continue this practice in different situations, I often receive wisdom regarding a course of action.

By breathing in the Spirit of Jesus in the middle of challenges, we allow Him to bring supernatural answers, needed wisdom, and necessary shifts. It's easy to get distracted and fall into emotional reactions, trying to forcefully achieve the outcome we desire. It's not that we are momentarily not born again, but rather, we are not breathing in fresh breath from Heaven, which is necessary for receiving divine intel. With the breath of God in us, we have access to the reality Paul wrote of in Acts 17:28: "For in him we live and move and have our being" (NIV). If our focus is on ourselves instead of Him, we aren't moving *in* Him.

While this may seem "out there" for some of you, I assure you, the practice of breathing in God's presence is in alignment with who God is. The very name of God, Yahweh, is spoken by each breath we inhale and exhale. YAH...WEH... I suppose one could argue with the question, "If every breath we breathe speaks His name, why isn't He intervening in every situation in the lives of every person? Why would it work sometimes and not all the time?" Good question.

The answer lies in the embrace. If we have embraced Jesus and taken hold of His name, He is in us, which makes us conquerors when we face troubles in this world! Situations may not go the way we think they should. Shifts may take longer than we like, but regardless of details, we have the Spirit of the almighty conqueror living inside of us. When we live from our embrace with Him and engage with Him as we breathe Him in, the atmosphere around us, along with the situations we face, can become remarkably different. Our pursuit should not be focused on what God can do for us, but instead on restoring and maintaining our connection and harmony with Him.

Breathing in Holy Spirit as described above is much like the "Breath Prayers" practiced by ancient saints to engage with God or a specific characteristic of His essence. For example, at times when peace is needed, we can close our eyes and focus on Jesus. We can say, "Yahweh," as we breathe in and, "Shalom," as we breathe out. It isn't necessary to say it out loud, but you can if you choose.

One of my favorite Breath Prayers is "I am in You, and You are in me." I envision myself *in* Him and Him *in* me as I breathe Him in and release what isn't from Him. Whatever your need, breathe Him in. Even if you don't have a specific need, you can simply take time to intentionally breathe in fresh breath from Heaven.

Our physical bodies need oxygen, and our spirits need His Spirit. Jesus is the breath of life, even more real and empowering than the air we breathe. He is everything we need. Embracing Him as He breathes upon us allows Him space to fulfill our needs by His Spirit. Sometimes, results come quickly; other times, it takes repetition. Either way, we are invited to *embrace and take hold of* Jesus as the Breath of God.

Points to Ponder

- Can you recall a time when you experienced Jesus as the Breath of Heaven? What shifted?
- Consider an area of your life that is currently in need of the Breath of God. What characteristic of God are you currently needing a greater measure of? Take a moment and receive more by simply breathing Him in.

Prayer of Embrace

Jesus, I acknowledge you as the Breath of Heaven. Thank You for Your breath that empowers me to function by Your Spirit throughout each day, revealing spiritual realities beyond my human understanding. Thank You for calming my spirit in the middle of chaos, bringing me into rhythm with Your heart, and filling me with wisdom as I breathe You in. I receive the breath of Yahweh, right now, Jesus, as You breathe on me. Amen.

Chapter 14

Feast of All Feasts

The purpose of the Lord's Supper is to receive
from Christ the nourishment and strength and hope and joy
that come from feasting our souls on all that He purchased
for us on the cross, especially His own fellowship.
**—John Piper, *Idolatry, the Lord's Supper,
and the Body of Christ*—**

We are celebrating the feast of the Eternal Birth which
God the Father has borne and never ceases to bear in all
eternity... But if it takes not place in me, what avails it?
Everything lies in this, that it should take place in me.
—Meister Eckhart, *Sermons & Treatises* —

For many, the word "feast" brings a picture to mind, like
a table full of favorite foods and surrounded by loved ones. Thanksgiving is an American holiday known for feasting. The Jewish culture
observes multiple feasts to celebrate their faith and to remember what
Yahweh has done for their ancestors throughout history. A feast can

celebrate a variety of occasions, and typically, those who indulge in a feast come away with their appetites satisfied and stomachs full.

Communion is a feast as well, and while our stomachs may not get filled by a small piece of bread and a sip of wine (or juice), there is a certain fullness that comes from celebrating Jesus' body and blood. Unfortunately, many believers seek superficial and nonessential "foods" to satisfy their spiritual hunger, not realizing they actually hunger for deeper communion with Jesus. Our physical body needs physical food and drink, but our spirit man needs spiritual sustenance that comes only through feasting on Jesus as the Bread and the Wine.

The Bread and Wine of Our Feast

The church I attended growing up had communion every Sunday. The Scripture was read, telling of what the elements represented, and from a young age, I participated with reverence. As my relationship with Jesus deepened, so did my reverence for communion. One day, while partaking, years after being born again, I encountered Jesus in a way that shifted my paradigm of His suffering.

I was alone in my kitchen, worshiping Him for His sacrifice. I began to pray something like "Thank You, Jesus, that in Your weakness, You were wounded for my transgressions and bore stripes for my healing." As the words were coming out of my mouth, I had a vision of His chest and arms. Both were sculpted with muscles, and I heard, *"It was My strength."* In that moment, I understood that it was in strength that He humbly yielded Himself to endure the vicious beating He received and then carried His cross to Calvary.

Jesus was surrounded by enemies when He was sentenced to death. Nevertheless, He was focused on the table His Father had prepared for Him—a feast with His beloved bride, made possible by His sacrifice. David wrote of this reality in Psalm 23:5: "You become my delicious feast even when my enemies dare to fight." Jesus feasted on the reality of redemption for His Bride. We feast on the same reality. Regardless of our enemies and their efforts to distract, deter, or even destroy us, we have a delicious feast set for us in the body and blood of our Savior.

Jesus spoke plainly regarding the feast He offers us:

- "Jesus said to them, 'I am the Bread of Life. Come every day to me and you will never be hungry. Believe in me and you will never be thirsty'" (John 6:35).
- "I am the true Bread of Life. Your ancestors ate manna in the desert and died. But standing here before you is the true Bread that comes out of heaven, and when you eat this Bread you will never die. I alone am this living Bread that has come to you from heaven. Eat this Bread and you will live forever. The living Bread I give you is my body, which I will offer as a sacrifice so that all may live" (John 6:48–51).
- "Eternal life comes to the one who eats my body and drinks my blood, and I will raise him up in the last day. For my body is real food for your spirit and my blood is real drink. The one who eats my body and drinks my blood lives in me and I live in him. The Father of life sent me, and he is my life. In the same way, the one who feeds upon me, I will become his life" (John 6:54–57).

Many who heard these words were perplexed and turned away, not able to comprehend or accept His words by faith. However, many remained, and multitudes continue to join in eating His body and drinking His blood.

Eating and Drinking the Feast

Just as we cannot live without water, we cannot have eternal life without drinking the blood of Jesus—coming into covenant with Him.

To drink of His blood is to be hydrated by the covenant. To eat of His flesh is to be nourished by all He provides through His body: strength, perseverance, endurance, forgiveness, and healing, to name a few. He is our sustenance. Eating His flesh and drinking His blood is to feast on Him.

When I eat the bread, I thank Him for His strength and receive it for myself as I envision Him enduring His flogging on my behalf. As I envision His back torn open by the whipping He received with leather cords embedded with pieces of metal and bone, I eat of His open flesh and thank Him for my healing. I thank Him for the freedom I have from mental anguish because of the wounding He received upon His brow and scalp from the crown of thorns. When I envision Him carrying the cross with a body weakened by torturous brutality, I eat of His perseverance. And when I see Him hanging on the cross in my mind's eye, each hand and foot fastened to the cross with crude nails, I eat of His body that was held there by His love for me.

Each time I drink the communion drink, I think of His blood that came through His pores as He suffered in agony in the Garden of Gethsemane. I think of the blood that poured from each of the wounds in His flesh. I drink the communion cup, thinking of His precious, sinless blood, the sacrifice He poured out to cleanse my conscience and free me from my dead works, so that I may live in union with Him. I remember His blood, the price He paid for my redemption, sealing me in covenant with Him. As I drink the cup, I receive His life, for life is in the blood.

Just as the taste of wine is determined by the country, region, field, and soil it is grown in, the blood wine of Jesus holds within it the nutrients of Heaven. The blood of Jesus contains God's DNA; each time we partake, we receive a transforming transfusion. The substance we receive is beyond the actual elements we consume; as we eat and drink of Him, we eat and drink His essence, who He is. Jesus is the feast that far surpasses all others.

There is a heavenly reality that transcends the reality of earth. Jesus spoke of this reality at the well in John 4. After speaking to the Samaritan woman, He told His disciples that He had food they didn't know about. There is a sustenance that comes by *knowing* Him the way He *knew* His Father. While we need earthly food to sustain our physical body, knowing Jesus as our bread and wine is what sustains our spirit man. As we taste this heavenly feast and its goodness, we develop an insatiable desire for more.

The Feast of God's Kingdom

As Jesus ate His last Passover meal with His disciples, He reiterated the mandate that He gave His followers in John 6 to eat His flesh and drink His blood.

> Then he told them, "I have longed with passion and desire to eat this Passover lamb with you before I endure my sufferings. I promise you that the next time we eat this, we will be together in the feast of God's kingdom." Then he raised a cup and gave thanks to God and said to them, "Take this and pass it on to one another and drink. I promise you that the next time we drink this wine, we will be together in the feast of God's kingdom." Then he lifted up a loaf, and after praying a prayer of thanksgiving to God, he gave each of his apostles a piece of bread, saying, "This loaf is my body, which is now being offered to you. Always eat it to remember me." After supper was over, he lifted the cup again and said, "This cup is my blood of the new covenant I make with you, and it will be poured out soon for all of you."

— Luke 22:15–20

We take Communion in remembrance of Christ's suffering and ought to do so often, but when we do, it is important to focus on Jesus' words: "The next time ... we will be together in the feast of God's kingdom." What exactly is the *feast of God's Kingdom?* The feast of God's Kingdom is the body and blood of Jesus. For that is how we enter the Kingdom of God—through His sacrifice as the Lamb of God. He established God's Kingdom with His death and resurrection, and it is now within us. We feast with Him, *together*, in the spiritual reality of God's Kingdom, as we feast on His body and blood.

Shortly after His resurrection, Jesus walked with the two disciples on the road to Emmaus and unveiled to them from the Scriptures the revelation of Himself. As He did, they feasted on God's Kingdom. The reality of Jesus as the bread of Heaven is our spiritual feast. Although their hearts burned while He fed their spirits, it wasn't until He blessed and broke bread for them that their eyes were opened and they realized it was Jesus. These two disciples testified to the others of "how Jesus was recognized by them when he broke the bread" (Luke 24:35).

Jesus continues to unveil Himself to us as we eat His body and drink His blood. We experience the fullness He provides by the spiritual reality of the feast of God's Kingdom. As we partake of His body as the bread of Heaven and His blood as the wine of the new covenant, we are *embracing and taking hold of* the Feast of all feasts.

Points to Ponder

- How has thinking of Jesus as your heavenly feast shifted your mindset regarding Communion?

- What spoke to you most in the discussion about focusing on
  the different aspects of Jesus' wounded body while taking
  Communion? Why?

Prayer of Embrace

*Thank You, Jesus, for offering Your body to receive my penalty,
sacrificing Your blood for my redemption, and sealing me in
covenant with You. Help me to receive the fullness of the feast
You have prepared for me. Reveal any distractions keeping me
from living in communion with You and feasting on all that
Your body and blood provide for me. I long to live from the
reality of the spiritual sustenance You provide. Amen.*

Chapter 15

Ultimate Example

Only by taking Jesus' example into every part
of our lives will we be able to win in life.
—Loren Cunningham, *Making Jesus Lord*—

Jesus stands absolutely alone in history; in teaching,
in example, in character, an exception, a marvel,
and He is Himself the evidence of Christianity.
—Arthur Tappan Pierson, *Many Infallible Proofs*—

A good teacher provides examples. In the learning process, it is always helpful to have an example of what to do or how to behave. It would be nearly impossible to do any learning assignment correctly without proper instructions to guide us. This is why classrooms have visual aids and instruction manuals include step-by-step pictures for items that require assembly.

In the same way, parents are examples for their children on how to function in daily life. Children learn how to care for themselves and others through their experience with their parents. They also learn how to interact relationally and conversationally from the example their parents provide. The lives of parents are like pictures that children learn from. Many find it difficult to know God, relate to Him, or have a relationship with Him because they haven't had good examples.

God's language is picture. The original Hebrew text is pictographs—communication through pictures. Jesus only taught in parables—word pictures. So it stands to reason that His human life is a picture, an example, of what it looks like to have a relationship with God as our Father.

I remember a time when one of my daughters was a toddler and reached an item from the shelf in the bathroom that was potentially hazardous. Each time I recall the words that came out of my mouth that day, I cringe. I said, "You should know better." Immediately, I heard Holy Spirit say, "She doesn't know better—she needs you to teach her." Of course, she did! How foolish of me to think a toddler should know the right thing to do without instruction. I don't remember the specifics, but I do remember that whatever she got into that day was from a desire to imitate her parents. That's what children do.

God's intention from the beginning was for His children to imitate Him. He fashioned us to walk with Him and live according to the image in which we were made: His. Adam and Eve walked and lived in union with God until they were deceived into choosing differently. Since their fall, humanity has struggled to see and hear God clearly. It seems that most humans prefer the ease of following others in the natural realm over training their senses to see and hear God in the spirit realm. This is why Jesus, quoting Isaiah, said,

> Although they listen carefully to everything I speak, they don't understand a thing I say. They look and pretend to see, but the eyes of their hearts are closed.

> Their minds are dull and slow to perceive, their ears
> are plugged and are hard of hearing, and they have
> deliberately shut their eyes to the truth. Otherwise
> they would open their eyes to see, and open their ears
> to hear, and open their minds to understand. Then
> they would turn to me and I would instantly heal them.
>
> — Matthew 13:14–15

Four Key Truths

Each human experiences true contentment when living like Jesus, in union and intimacy with God, according to their divine design. While the specific details of each of our lives differ, we can follow Jesus' example of total surrender to God's Kingdom and will by living according to four key truths that John recorded in his Gospel.

1. Jesus did nothing from Himself or of His own initiative.

"So Jesus said, 'I speak to you eternal truth. The Son is unable to do anything from himself or through his own initiative'" (John 5:19).

2. Jesus only did what He saw the Father do.

"I only do the works that I see the Father doing, for the Son does the same works as his Father" (John 5:19).

3. Jesus only spoke what He heard the Father speak.

"For I'm not speaking as someone who is self-appointed, but I speak by the authority of the Father himself who sent me, and who instructed me what to say. And I know that the

Father's commands result in eternal life, and that's why I speak the very words I've heard him speak" (John 12:50).

4. Anyone who looked at Jesus saw the Father.

"Jesus replied, 'Philip, I've been with you all this time and you still don't know who I am? How could you ask me to show you the Father, for anyone who has looked at me has seen the Father'" (John 14:9).

These truths reveal that Jesus saw, heard, and existed beyond the earthly realm and into the spirit realm. Because of this, He was able to keep His eyes focused on the Father while living out His earthly experience. The life of Jesus demonstrated the nature and character of God the Father as He showed us God's ways and communicated God's thoughts. Jesus lived the reality of the prayer He taught His disciples: "Manifest your kingdom realm, and cause your every purpose to be fulfilled on earth, just as it is in heaven" (Matthew 6:10). God's Kingdom realm was manifested in the life of Jesus and His every purpose was fulfilled in Him.

Now, let's take an in-depth look at each of these key truths and how they empower us.

Nothing from Himself or of His Own Initiative

To some, it may have seemed that Jesus did take initiative and do things His own way because His way was foreign to what they had been taught. It may have seemed He worked alone because He didn't have a human mentor. But He did nothing from Himself. Jesus lived from His union with the Father, which is the reality that Paul wrote about in Romans 8:14 when he said, "The mature children of God are those who are moved by the impulses of the Holy Spirit."

What Would Jesus Do and Say?

There was a movement in the 90s that encouraged believers to ponder the question, "What Would Jesus Do?" There were silicone bracelets of all colors with the letters WWJD on the wrists of Christians everywhere. While the movement has passed, this question is still worth pondering in our daily lives. If we were made to imitate our Father in Heaven and Jesus only did what He saw the Father doing, then it only makes sense to do what Jesus did. If Jesus only spoke what He heard the Father speak, all of God's children should do the same.

Seeing the Father

What an amazing thought. Every person who looked at Jesus was seeing the Father. Every action, every conversation, every decision, every teaching, and all His mannerisms were a reflection of the Father through Him. We don't have Jesus with us in the flesh to see Him the way people did when He was on earth, and there isn't a book that provides the specifics of what to do or say in every given situation. However, there is a book that teaches us the nature and character of Jesus, which is the nature and character of the Father— the Bible.

As we read and reread the Gospels, our understanding of who Jesus is deepens. We can see how kind and merciful He was, especially in the way He associated with sinners and outcasts. He embodied love and was driven by compassion. Jesus embraced the forsaken and was unafraid to touch the unclean as He healed their diseases. When presented with obvious and blatant sin, He revealed His purpose to rescue the lost by not being judgmental or condemning. He was patient when the disciples were slow to understand and provided revelation when they asked. Through the life of Jesus and the lens of Scripture, we can see the Father.

Learning from Jesus

Though Jesus was full of compassion and love, He did speak strongly to some people: the self-righteous religious leaders. They were caught up in pride and arrogance, upholding man-made traditions over God's Law. Jesus didn't beat around the bush when He addressed them and refused to allow their preconceived ideas about Messiah to influence His obedience to the Father. When people didn't accept His answer, He didn't beg them to. He honored the free will of people, allowing the consequence of their choice to reject Him.

Jesus demonstrated a life of prayer, slipping away early in the mornings to spend time alone with His Father. He experienced grief, anger, and joy. He not only preached forgiveness but demonstrated it, receiving the kiss of betrayal from Judas and interceding for those driving the nails into His hands and feet. Jesus was able to reveal the heart of the Father in all things and endure and persevere through His trials because of His intimate relationship with the Father. He lived in and from His presence.

The example Jesus offers us goes beyond what I can relate within these pages, and quite frankly, beyond the pages of Scripture. John testified at the end of his Gospel that the world wouldn't have enough room to contain the books written of all that Jesus did while on earth.[1] If the works He did were too numerous to record, surely there were more teachings than what was recorded. However, there is one who knows all things, and He lives inside each of us who has opened our hearts to Him.

Jesus knows our situations and the decisions before us. He still teaches those who have a desire to learn. All we need to do is pause and ask Him, "Jesus, what would You do?" or "Jesus, what would You say?"

Oftentimes, when I need guidance, I ask Him to show me what to do or say through His Word. Within moments, He brings a passage of

Scripture to mind, revealing the principle of that passage as my guidance. Other times, He guides me with an image of myself doing something. Many other times, I hear a whisper in my spirit, giving instructions or words to speak. I believe this is part of what it looks like for us to follow Jesus' example: not taking our own initiative, only doing what the Father does, only saying what He says, and revealing Him to others.

Living in Union

Jesus told Nicodemus that, "No one has risen into the heavenly realm except the Son of Man who also exists in heaven" (John 3:13). Jesus, the Son of Man, walked on earth in a human body while existing in heaven simultaneously. This is easy for most of us to accept, after all, He was God in the flesh. But have you considered His prayer in John 17:24: "Father, I ask that you allow everyone that you have given to me to be with me where I am!" He wasn't talking about when we die! Jesus was asking the Father to grant us access to the heavenly realm while still in the natural realm. Paul speaks of this reality in Ephesians 2:6: "we are now co-seated as one with Christ!"

The gospels contain many examples of how to live like Jesus, but there is more to it than just doing and saying what He does and says. Jesus is the blueprint for the new creation life: living in union with the Father. Life union is what empowered Jesus to live in both realms. Always seeing and hearing the Father and revealing Him to others. This is the example He is calling us to follow. Life union positions us in the Father since we are in Jesus, and He is one with the Father. We must live from this awareness. Recognizing and refusing distractions, along with our ideas and opinions, and instead looking and listening for what the Father is doing and saying.

Our relationship with the Father, through Jesus, is meant to direct our daily life. Jesus not only showed us the way, He is *the only* way to life-union with the Father. He lived obediently to the Father in all things, while displaying the very nature and character of God. We must become more like Him each day—yielding to Him and His ways and *embracing and taking hold of* Jesus as the Ultimate Example of a life fully surrendered to the Father.

Points to Ponder

- In what area of your life could you better follow Jesus' example?
- Ask Holy Spirit to show you a passage or story from Scripture that reveals the Father's heart concerning this area. What did He show you?
- How often do you pause to ask Jesus what He would do or say? What action can you take to be more intentional in seeking His example?

Prayer of Embrace

Jesus, Thank You for revealing the Father in all that You do and say. I confess that I haven't sought Your wisdom or Your will in all things. Forgive me for the times I have acted from my own ideas and spoken from my own opinion. Help me to live from my seat in the heavenly realm while living on earth; may my spiritual eyes and ears be open continually as I live in life-union with You. I choose to embrace and take hold of You as my ultimate example. Amen.

Chapter 16

Rest

When the heart submits, then Jesus reigns.
When Jesus reigns, there is rest.
**—James Hudson Taylor, *Union and
Communion*—**

We shall never find happiness by looking at
our prayers, our doings, or our feelings; it is what Jesus is,
not what we are, that gives rest to the soul.
—Charles Spurgeon, *Morning by Morning*—

MANY OF US IN THE BODY OF CHRIST ARE LADEN WITH STRESS
and tension from the tasks of daily life. When it comes to accomplishing the mission and mandate given to us by God, we can be deceived into believing that we must conjure up our own strength to do so. It is easy to get caught up in striving to overcome challenges. Too often we think that we must figure things out on our own and do it just right to be accepted by or acceptable to God. This is a "works mentality"—thinking we have to fix ourselves and make God's plan for our lives come to pass. If we are striving under a belief system that

says, "it all depends on me," it's no wonder so many of us are full of stress and worry.

Rest is often considered a time to chill out, relax, do something enjoyable, or do nothing at all. These views are accurate but are focused on the natural realm. There is also a rest available for our spirit as we go about daily life.

Until recent years, my understanding was that rest for Christians meant doing no work all day on a specific day of the week. That isn't wrong, but again, it's focused on the natural realm, and the rest God has for us goes much deeper. As we live in union with Him, with our hearts at peace, we experience the faith-rest Jesus purchased for us on Calvary.

Created for Rest

Humanity was created to function from a place of rest. In the Genesis account of creation, God worked for six days, creating the earth and all that is in it. Since mankind was created last, all that was needed to sustain life had been provided for us by our loving Creator. The work was done. When Adam received the breath of God in his lungs and became a living being, he began his life in rest, surrounded by the goodness of God. All that he needed was already prepared.

Even though God had given Adam "work" to do, that work was to tend, from a place of rest, all that had been created for him. After Adam disobeyed, he was then told to work by the sweat of his brow. In this context, I see "tend" as representing the work we do while living in union with the Father.

When we tend a garden, the plants are already seeded and growing. We help them grow by the care we provide or hinder their growth by a lack of care. It is the same with the work God calls us to do. He already has all the details worked out; the seeds are in the ground, so to speak. Our part is to come into alignment with His plan and tend to what He has established.

However, when we choose to live outside of union with the Father, it is easy to get caught up in striving and self-effort. Self-effort is focused on ourselves—trying to make things come together according to our initiative, our thoughts, and opinions. When we strive in this way, our work reveals our abilities and talents instead of revealing the Father. I've noticed that whenever I become self-focused, I experience an internal wrestle. I become anxious and worried about my performance because I am not at rest.

Striving in self-effort is exhausting. Thankfully, God has invited us into His rest.

Promise of Rest

Years ago, as I studied the presence of God, I meditated on God's answer to Moses in Exodus 33 for days and received one of the most profound revelations about rest. Moses had told God that an angel of the Lord wasn't enough. After experiencing God's presence, Moses simply wouldn't go forward without Him. God answered Moses, promising, "My presence will go with you *and* I will give you rest" (Exodus 33:14 NIV, emphasis added).

This verse captured my spirit, and I was drawn back to it over and over. What stuck out to me was that Moses hadn't asked for rest—he had asked for God's presence. It seems clear from this verse that rest was and is a priority to God. If He wanted to gift Moses with rest when he was seeking His presence, I believe it is safe to say He desires to give rest to all those seeking His Presence. God's plan and design from the beginning was for mankind to live *in* His presence *from* the place of rest.

The word "rest" in Exodus 33:14 means to settle down, dwell, and remain. God was taking His people into a Promised Land of abundance and peace, but He had and still has an even greater plan. He wants us in a far superior resting place: Christ. His desire from the beginning has been for His people to dwell in Him and remain at rest.

The rest of God doesn't eliminate work, though. The Israelites still had to go forward in faith and conquer obstacles between them and their inheritance. Their feet had to carry them, and their arms had to defend them, but first, their hearts had to believe. In the same way, there is work for us to do, but we are to do it with a believing heart from the position of rest.

We have the responsibility to get up each day and do the plethora of works He has prepared for each of us. The list is endless as to where our feet carry us and the type of work we do with our hands; however, as lovers of God, we are invited to do it all from a place of rest.

Entering Rest

Hebrews 3:9–11 tells of God's grief over the Israelites' inability to enter the rest He had for them. He had done so many miracles of provision for His people, revealing His love and trustworthiness. Witnessing His miraculous provision ought to have given them confident faith to rest in God's care as they obeyed His instructions, yet the Israelites refused to learn His ways. "So God swore an oath that they would never enter into his calming place of rest all because they disobeyed him" (Hebrews 3:18).

Wouldn't it be horrible to see the mighty hand of God miraculously deliver you from your oppressive tyrant and provide all you need for forty years and then not enter His rest because you have a hard, stubborn heart? Sadly, so many of us have the same struggle that the Israelites did. We may not be walking circles in an actual desert, but metaphorically, many believers experience the goodness of God daily but have wandering hearts that refuse to learn God's ways because His ways don't align with their preconceived ideas.

If it were all about entering a geographical location to rest in, then this section in Hebrews wouldn't necessarily apply to us, but chapter 4 provides us with the true spiritual message.

> Now the promise of entering into God's rest is still for us today. So we must be extremely careful to ensure that we all embrace the fullness of that promise and not fail to experience it. ... For those of us who believe, faith activates the promise and we experience the realm of confident rest! ... Those who first heard the good news of deliverance failed to enter into that realm of faith's rest because of their unbelieving hearts. Yet the fact remains that we still have the opportunity to enter into the faith-rest life and experience the fulfillment of the promise!
>
> — Hebrews 4:1, 3, 6

The promise is about entering His rest, a realm that is obtained by faith.

> Now if this promise of "rest" was fulfilled when Joshua brought the people into the land, God wouldn't have spoken later of another "rest" yet to come. So we conclude that there is still a full and complete Sabbath-rest waiting for believers to experience. As we enter into God's faith-rest life we cease from our own works, just as God celebrates his finished works and rests in them. So then we must be eager to experience this faith-rest life, so that no one falls short by following the same pattern of doubt and unbelief.

— Hebrews 4:8–11

Again, rest doesn't imply that we don't do any work. Instead, we work from a place of faith and rest, believing that God has already done the work in the spirit realm. Our part is to simply partner with Him by aligning with the destiny He created us for. By doing so, we activate the manifestation of our destiny in the natural realm. The only way to *not* enter rest is to refuse to learn His ways because of an unbelieving heart.

Jesus Is Our Rest

God the Father promised rest to those who would believe in Him, and Jesus made it clear that no one could come to the Father except through Him.[1] It stands to reason, then, that the only way to enter rest is Jesus. In fact, in Matthew 11:28–30 Jesus told His hearers, "Are you weary, carrying a heavy burden? Come to me. I will refresh your life, for I am your oasis. Simply join your life with mine. Learn my ways and you'll discover that I'm gentle, humble, easy to please. You will find refreshment and rest in me. For all that I require of you will be pleasant and easy to bear."

Previous to Jesus inviting people to find rest in Him, He had acknowledged that He and His ways didn't fit people's expectations. He responded to some criticism in verse 19, saying, "But God's wisdom will become visible by those who embrace it." It may not have seemed too wise to the Israelites to leave Goshen, where their ancestors had prospered for so long. They may have assumed their deliverer was going to come and overthrow Pharaoh and empower them to rule over those who had enslaved them. And when the wilderness experience presented so many challenges, they obviously struggled to see God's wisdom.

Similarly, the religious leaders and many others in Jesus' day struggled to see God's wisdom. They struggled to believe that Jesus was the Messiah because He didn't fit their preconceived idea. It seems evident they were focused on the natural realm, expecting a conquering king who would overthrow Rome. Like the Israelites of Moses' day, they may have been anticipating a time when they would be able to repay the evil they suffered at the hands of wicked rulers.

How many of us struggle with understanding God's ways, becoming frustrated when our dreams and plans to achieve great things for God don't pan out? How many of us experience hardships and suffering at the hands of the wicked and struggle to comprehend God's ways of dealing with those responsible? These are very real and legitimate struggles, for which He offers us rest. The answers lie in God's wisdom, which is attained by faith. His ways don't make sense according to the wisdom of the world. First, we must embrace His wisdom, no matter how nonsensical it may seem, then we see it—if not immediately, eventually.

To enter God's rest, we must enter union with Jesus and yield to learning His ways instead of trying to convince Him to do it our way. It is when we embrace His ways in faith that we experience the refreshment and rest that our soul so desperately needs. Regardless of the Israelites' lack of understanding, Moses had encountered and believed in the necessity of the manifest presence of God. He believed so deeply that he was willing to forfeit the promised inheritance rather than be without God's presence. It was because of his belief that God promised the rest that comes with His presence.

Jesus is the manifest presence of God. Rest is the essence of who He is. When He and the disciples were in a boat with winds and waves threatening their lives, Jesus was asleep.[2] He was totally at peace. This is a picture to ponder. We can experience this reality in our lives. When the winds and waves of troubles and challenges, upsets and disappointments, and pains and sorrows surround us, we can hold onto Jesus. He holds the solution, and He is our source of encouragement and healing. No matter the situation, He is in the boat with us, and He invites us into His rest.

We are meant to do all that we have been fashioned for from a place of rest. If people or situations seem to bring hindrances to the pursuit of our purpose, we can rest. If we face delay or if our plans don't unfold according to our expectations, we can rest. If the dreams in our heart take a detour and we have to surrender our preconceived ideas, we can rest. Regardless of the specifics, we have a *faith-rest life* available to us in Christ. We simply join our life with His.

Just as God did all the work to provide sustainable life for mankind, Jesus did all the work for us to enter back into the rest that Father God fashioned us to live from. Since unbelieving hearts don't enter the rest of God, let's be determined to live a life of faith, living in union with Jesus, believing His Word, and trusting His ways. As His children, we are given authority to live and function from His rest in all that He has commissioned us to do. The way to unlock this reality is to *embrace and take hold of* Him as Rest.

Points to Ponder

- In what area of your life are you struggling to align with rest?
- Ask Holy Spirit to reveal His wisdom for that area. What did He show you?
- Is there a specific burden Jesus is asking you to lay down in order to learn His way?

Prayer of Embrace

Father, forgive me for the times I have doubted Your ways. Help me to yield to Your wisdom even when it doesn't make sense to me. I don't want to live in the pain caused by what I have experienced, and I don't want to live under the burden of stress from trying to accomplish Your will on my own. I desire to live in true rest, the rest you have for me in the spirit realm. Jesus, increase my measure of faith as I open my heart to You as Rest. Help me to join my life with You in every area so that I may experience the refreshment and rest that are only found in You. Amen.

Chapter 17

King Eternal

This King, full of goodness and mercy,
lovingly embraces me, seats me at his table,
waits on me himself, gives me the keys to his
treasures and treats me in all things as his favorite.
—Brother Lawrence—

The gospel is not about choosing to follow advice,
it's about being called to follow a King. Not just someone
with the power and authority to tell you what needs to be
done but someone with the power and authority to do what
needs to be done, and then to offer to you as good news.
—Timothy J. Keller, *Jesus the King Study Guide*—

Loyalty and mercy, truth and faithfulness, protect the king,
And he upholds his throne by lovingkindness.
—Proverbs 20:28 AMP—

FEW PROMINENT HISTORICAL RULERS SERVE AS MODELS OF
virtuous kingship. For most of us, at least in America, our examples

are mainly limited to Disney's fairy tale kings and modern-day leaders who are self-seeking and rule harshly. This can create a lack of understanding and trust when relating to Jesus as King. Taking time to reflect on the nature of kingship and the significance of Jesus as King will enable us to discern whether He truly reigns in our lives and if we desire to be citizens of His Kingdom.

The Essence of Kingship

A king is a man who rules over a marked territory, such as a region or country.[1] Men who become kings are born into a royal family and inherit their position as ruler when their father, the previous king, dies. As king, he is the ultimate authority of his kingdom and rules over everyone within the set boundaries of his domain.

A king decrees the laws and determines the consequences of disobedience. He selects and empowers people he trusts to assist him in governing and overseeing the kingdom. The condition of his heart sets the atmosphere throughout the land he rules. People living under the rulership of a kind-hearted and generous king with goodwill toward humanity typically revere him and are blessed with an enjoyable life filled with abundance.

However, if the king is a selfish, greedy, power-hungry man, the people within his kingdom are most likely oppressed and poor and may even suffer violence under his leadership. The movie *The Lion King*[2] is a good example of how a king's heart impacts the people in his kingdom. Under the leadership of Mufasa, the entire region was prosperous, food and water were plentiful, and he carefully guarded the well-being of those under his domain.

Mufasa's jealous brother, Scar, on the other hand, had evil in his heart and thirsted for power. His selfish and evil actions brought death to Mufasa and caused fear and harm to those he ruled over. Scar's rule didn't last long, though. Mufasa's son, Simba, rose with a heart of courage and overthrew him. Simba was the rightful heir of the kingdom, and he ruled with the same authority, character, and goodwill as his father.

World history confirms what Disney has portrayed. Many books chronicle world history, recounting tales of kings and their kingdoms. One of those books is the Holy Bible, and within its pages are many accounts of kings, good and bad. God established the first king of Israel at the request of His people in 1 Samuel 8–10. God had already established His Son as King Eternal, which I will share shortly; however, the people didn't trust the ways of God, so He gave them what they asked for.

God's intention and hope was that each of Israel's kings who reigned would do so from a personal relationship with Him, seeking Him as Moses, Joshua, and Samuel had. The first one, although chosen by God, did not live in close relationship with Him. King Saul succumbed to the deceitfulness of the self-life and disobeyed God's instructions. David was chosen as Saul's successor, not because of stature or having come from a royal lineage, but because of his heart. David pursued God in all matters.

While David was human and imperfect like the rest of us and fell prey to the deceitfulness of the self-life at times, he quickly repented and turned back to God with a humble heart when he failed. God honored David for his deep devotion to Him by having Jesus come through his family line.

This fulfilled the promise God made in 1 Chronicles 17:11–14 that He would raise up one of David's offspring to succeed him and be set over his house and kingdom forever. While his son Solomon was his successor and built the temple, God was speaking of Jesus being of David's lineage. Solomon's kingdom ended when he died. However, Jesus lives forever, He is over God's house and kingdom forever, and His throne has been established...forever.[3]

Jesus Is King

Jesus never proclaimed Himself as King while He was on earth, but He also didn't deny it. When Pilate asked him in Luke 23:3, "Is this true? Are you their king and Messiah?" Jesus answered, "It is true." According to our earthly understanding and the above definition of a king, it doesn't make sense that Jesus didn't let everyone know who He was and make them obey and submit to His authority.

But Jesus didn't operate from an earthly nature., He didn't come to force people into submission., He came to reveal the eternal purpose of God and prove what truth really is. He operates from the heavenly realm, holding all power and authority. Earth is set in the cosmos and is only a part of God's endless expanse. What Jesus has to offer is far superior to what we experience here.

Throughout the Gospel of John, Jesus spoke to His followers and the religious leaders about "eternal truth."[4] Each time, He expounded with revelations about the heavenly Kingdom. Kings of this world force people to live according to their prescribed way of life. Jesus *invites* us into His. He does have set ways, but whether we live according to His Kingdom or not is a matter of the heart and a freewill choice. The eternal Kingdom of God is available to all mankind, but entrance for each individual hinges on accepting Jesus as King.

The Type of King That Jesus Is

King Eternal

In Psalm 2, we read the words quoted by the Son of "God-Enthroned ... the Sovereign One" (v. 4). He declares, "I will reveal the eternal purpose of God. For he has decreed over me, 'You are my favored

Son. And as your Father I have crowned you as my King Eternal. Today I became your Father. I myself have poured out my King on Zion, my holy mountain'" (v. 7). This is Jesus speaking in the heavenly realm before He came in the flesh.

Matthew 3:17 makes it clear that Jesus is the one God crowned King Eternal, "Then suddenly the voice of the Father shouted from the sky, saying, 'This is my Son—the Beloved! My greatest delight is in him.'" The Hebrew word for "king" in Psalm 2 comes from a root word that means to reign and to ascend the throne from the beginning. God, our sovereign creator, established Jesus as King Eternal from the inception of His plan to create the earth and the cosmos. Jesus was already King when He was planted as a seed in the womb of Mary, and He will remain King throughout eternity because He conquered death and lives eternally.

King of Glory

"So wake up, you living gateways! Lift up your heads, you doorways of eternity! Welcome the King of Glory, for he is about to come through you" (Psalm 24:7). We are the living gateways and the doorways of eternity. Jesus, the King of Glory, stands at the door of our hearts, waiting to come in and through us.

In Jesus' prayer to the Father in John 17:5, He addressed His glory: "So my Father, restore me back to the glory that we shared together when we were face-to-face before the universe was created." And again, in verse 10, He stated, "My glory is revealed through their surrendered lives." And in verse 22, Jesus declared, "For the very glory you have given to me I have given them."

We don't have to wait until we die and go to Heaven to experience His glory. He wants us to open our hearts, our gates, and our doorways, and let Him *and* His glory come in and through us to the world around us. As the King of Glory, Jesus takes us from one level of glory to another. Each time He draws us closer to Him, we become more like Him and arise to a new level of glory.[5]

King of Kings

While there have been countless kings throughout history, Jesus is the King of kings.

- "Yes, God will make his appearing in his own divine timing, for he is the exalted God, the only powerful One, the King over every king, and the Lord of power!" (1 Timothy 6:15).
- "On his robe and on his thigh he had inscribed a name: King of kings and Lord of lords" (Revelation 19:16).

In times past, I thought "King of kings" pointed to the fact that Jesus was King over all the kings that have ruled on earth, such as the kings listed in the Bible, the kings of England, France, and Spain, as well as all dictators, emperors, presidents, prime ministers, and the like. Then one day, I read and pondered Revelation 1:5–6: "To him who loves us and has freed us from our sins by his blood and *made us kings* and priests to his God and Father, to him be glory and dominion forever and ever" (emphasis added).

He made us kings! Peter spoke of this truth as well: "But you are God's chosen treasure—priests *who are kings*, a spiritual 'nation' set apart as God's devoted ones" (1 Peter 2:9, emphasis added). He has made every believer who has yielded to His authority and transforming power to be a king under His kingship. As kings under King Jesus, He empowers us to rule and reign with Him. Our role is to govern with Him and bring Heaven to earth by living and decreeing His Word and by loving others as He does.

Each of us is invited into His Kingdom to enjoy eternal life, but going to Heaven when we die isn't the only purpose for embracing Jesus as

King. As citizens of His Kingdom, we are to live according to His character and nature to establish His Kingdom on earth as one of the kings under the King of kings. He has graciously given us His righteousness and His glory. As we open our hearts and allow Him to come into us and through us, He transforms us from the inside out to become more like Him. We then transform the world around us by "ruling" our atmospheres with the love and goodness of God.

King-Priest

Kings rule over a region, and priests intercede for others. Under the Law of Moses, the priests presented offerings and sacrifices to God to make atonement for their sins and those of the people. All priests were from the tribe of Levi. Hebrews 7 tells of Melchizedek, priest of the Most High God, the King of Peace. His name means "king of righteousness."[6] He "has no father or mother, and no record of any of his ancestors. He was never born and he never died, but his life is like a picture of the Son of God, a King-Priest forever!" (Hebrews 7:3).

The priesthood of Melchizedek existed before and supersedes the Levitical priesthood. Jesus came in the likeness of Melchizedek. He wasn't from the tribe of Levi, and His priesthood "did not arise because of a genealogical right under the law to be a priest, but by the power of an indestructible, resurrection life" (Hebrews 7:16). He finished the sacrificial system, once and for all, when He offered Himself on the cross, paying the debt of all humanity.

All priests under the old system eventually died,[7] but Jesus lives forever, so He is forever able to save everyone who comes to God through Him. Jesus interceded for us by being the once and for all sacrifice and He is forever making intercession for us as our High Priest.[8] "God affirmed his royal priesthood with his promise, saying, The Lord has made a solemn oath and will never change his mind, 'You are a King-Priest forever!'" (Hebrews 7:21).

As King, Jesus rules in righteousness and peace; as Priest, He is always interceding for us. His intercession fills the gaps in our lives, and He forever presents His blood to the Father on our behalf. What better king could there be than this majestic King-Priest?

Indestructible, Invisible, Full of Glory

King Jesus is worthy of the highest honors. Paul knew this by personal experience: "Because of this my praises rise to the King of all the universe who is indestructible, invisible, and full of glory, the only God who is worthy of the highest honors throughout all of time and throughout the eternity of eternities! Amen!" (1 Timothy 1:17).

This is Jesus! Indestructible—He cannot be destroyed, nor can His work of uniting us to God. Invisible—we can't see Him with our natural, earthly eyes. Seeing our King of kings requires our spiritual sight. But once we see Him, truly see Him, there is no possibility of unseeing Him. Jesus is rapturous, and as we covered above, He is full of glory.

Jesus as King of Our Lives

Practically speaking, what does it look like, or what does it mean to have Jesus as King? It means we have given our hearts over to His Kingdom rule. This statement can be difficult to accept for some since we live in a corrupt world where many people have suffered injustice at the hands of corrupt rulers. Whether those rulers were governmental authorities or rather family members, teachers, coaches, pastors, or any other leader who was supposed to be trustworthy, if they mistreated us, they all represent a ruler of sorts who abused their position. This is not true of Jesus.

Jesus is trustworthy, and He does not abuse His authority. He created the world as a realm with set boundaries and rules by which to live.

Under Jesus' rule, we obey His commandments. His commandments are not burdensome; they simply guide us to live according to the way we were designed. He also has promises of heavenly treasures that far outweigh earthly treasures, and, while many receive abundant blessings on earth, such blessings are not guaranteed, nor are they a mark of success or rank in the Kingdom of God.

As King, Jesus desires to bless those who choose to be citizens of His Kingdom. His kingship is more about His love for us than it is about our love for Him. Jesus is a good king, and He rules from the fruit of His Spirit, the essence of who He is. He cannot contradict Himself.

On earth, people can live within a kingdom, obeying the set laws, but secretly despise their rulers or leaders. Not so with God's Kingdom. He knows what is in our hearts, and simply following His commands doesn't make us a citizen. What is in our hearts ultimately reveals the kingdom we belong to.

Living Under the King's Domain

Jesus didn't promote Himself as King on earth because He is King Eternal and the earth is temporal. His Kingdom is of the heavenly realm. His ways are higher than our ways and don't make sense to those fixed on an earthly mindset.

From the start until the end of His ministry on earth, Jesus proclaimed the Kingdom of God. Mark 1:14–15 tells us that Jesus "preached the wonderful gospel of God's Kingdom. His message was this: 'At last the fulfillment of the age has come! It is time for God's Kingdom to be experienced in its fullness! Turn your lives back to God and put your trust in the hope-filled gospel!'"

In Luke 4:43, Jesus told those begging Him to stay in Capernaum, "Don't you know there are other places I must go and offer the hope of God's Kingdom? This is what I have been sent to do." He continued the message of John the Baptist: "Keep turning away from your sins and come back to God" (Matthew 3:2 and Matthew 4:17). However, John said that "Heaven's kingdom was *about* to appear" (Matthew 3:1); Jesus declared, "Heaven's kingdom realm is *now* accessible" (Matthew 4:17, emphasis added).

Since His Kingdom realm is accessible, that means it is within reach, and we can grab hold of it and take it as ours. Entering Heaven's Kingdom realm begins with forsaking evil, along with our way of thinking and living. It requires action, but we must guard against focusing on the outward. Our heart is where true *turning* takes place. Strictly adhering to religious traditions and doctrine doesn't prove repentance, nor does doing good works.

Paul taught that "the kingdom of God is not a matter of rules about food and drink, but is in the realm of the Holy Spirit, filled with righteousness, peace, and joy" (Romans 14:17). Paul was teaching that entering the Kingdom of God is only possible by being born of the Spirit of God, not by strict adherence to rituals and feasts. His words are to us as well. We must go beyond the natural realm and live in the realm of righteousness, peace, and joy with Holy Spirit.

Jesus connected righteousness to the Kingdom of God in Matthew 6:33, saying, "So above all, constantly seek God's kingdom and his righteousness, then all these less important things will be given to you abundantly." God is righteous. Righteousness is the standard of His Kingdom. In simple terms, to be righteous means we are in right standing with God, living according to His virtues and characteristics, such as kindness and goodness, in our personal and public relationships.

It may seem contradictory to quote Paul, who said the Kingdom of God isn't about rules, and simultaneously say that being a part of God's Kingdom means choosing to live according to His rules. I assure you, it's not. Paul was addressing a false belief that following rules granted entrance to the Kingdom of God. On the contrary, we

146

enter by believing in Jesus and receiving Holy Spirit by faith. We follow His rules because of our love for Him.

It is from a heart of love that we embrace Jesus as King and from a heart of love that we humbly yield to His ways and His commands. Jesus told His disciples, "Loving me empowers you to obey my word" (John 14:23). When His ways don't make sense and fail our expectations, or when our flesh nature struggles to live according to His ways, our love for Him empowers us.

The people of Israel, specifically the religious leaders, rejected Jesus as their King because He didn't fit their expectations. They were offended by His teachings and the revelation He brought of God and His Kingdom. How many of us have done the same in one way or another?

There will come a time when King Jesus will appear on His throne of splendor and separate the sheep and goats. The sheep, those who know His voice and follow Him, will be placed on His right side, the place of authority. To these, Jesus will say, "You have a special place in my Father's heart. Come and experience the full inheritance of the kingdom realm that has been destined for you from before the foundation of the world!" (Matthew 25:34).

The goats, those who look very similar to sheep but don't know His voice or follow Him, will be placed on the left and sent to the eternal fire. The religious leaders could be considered goats. They looked righteous with all their rule-following and devotion to rituals, but their hearts were not righteous. They were hungry for power and fixated on earthly, temporal matters, unfamiliar with the Kingdom of Heaven.

As Jesus walked on earth in bodily form, He lived from and by the Spirit of God, displaying and revealing the love and mercy of God. He embodied His Kingdom of righteousness, peace, and joy. Jesus is King of His Kingdom, and, as kings do, He has a throne. His throne, however, isn't in a far-off place. His throne is the heart of every human. The question is whether or not we grant Him permission to be seated there. To be a part of the Kingdom of God requires enthroning Jesus as King of our hearts, which results in living according to His righteous rule.

Jesus is a trustworthy and faithful King whose ways are good; He rules according to His character and has an abundance of heavenly treasure for us to explore as we yield to Him. He is actively at work fulfilling His mandate to reveal the eternal purpose of God by His Spirit in and through us. He invites us to partner with Him in establishing His Kingdom on earth. This indestructible and invisible King Eternal, King of Glory, and King of kings has provided all we need to enter His Kingdom. We simply need to *embrace and take hold of King Jesus.*

Points to Ponder

- What detail about the kingship of Jesus stands out to you the most? Why?
- Is there an area in your life that you struggle to yield to the rulership of Jesus? Take some time to explore the reason why, and then invite Jesus to be enthroned in that area and to reveal His trustworthiness.
- Have you seen yourself as a king governing with King Jesus before? How does this view change your outlook concerning your time on earth?

Prayer of Embrace

Thank You, Jesus, for being a good and loving king who rules according to Your character and nature. Thank You for Your Kingdom of righteousness, peace, and joy. I worship You and am in awe of Your glorious splendor. Jesus, I choose to yield to You as king of my heart and live according to Your Kingdom reality, focusing on the eternal, heavenly realm. Help me grow in understanding how to govern with You to bring a greater manifestation of Your glory on the earth. Amen.

Chapter 18

Twofold Fire

I will put my fiery hand upon you
and purify you with fire into something clean.
—Isaiah 1:25—

In the same way that gold and silver are refined by fire,
the Lord purifies your heart by the tests and trials of life.
—Proverbs 17:3—

I have come to set the earth on fire, and how I wish it
were already ablaze with fiery passion for God!
—Luke 12:49—

YEARS AGO, WHEN I WAS YOUNG IN THE LORD, I TOOK A ROAD trip to the Bible belt with my mom and younger brother. While inquiring about a room at a hotel, I came upon a young man working a service desk who asked me if I knew Jesus. As I nodded in response, His gaze seemed to pierce the depths of my soul. He went on to ask if I had been baptized by fire. Sheepishly, I shook my head, having never heard of such a thing. What did that even mean? After asking permission, he prayed for me. All the while, I wondered if something like lightning would hit me. It didn't.

Before Jesus started His ministry, John the Baptist had declared that the one coming after Him would, as most translations read, "baptize with the Holy Spirit and with fire" (Matthew 3:11). What exactly is this baptism of fire, and what is its purpose? Whatever it is, it is linked with Holy Spirit, and Jesus is the source, and it is what this chapter is going to explore.

Facets of Fire

Fire is more than a flame that offers light and heat. Fire can also refer to burning passion, liveliness of imagination, and inspiration, which is why we say someone is "on fire for the Lord" when they express a great amount of zeal for Jesus. Some even feel the tangible presence of God as a burning sensation in their hands or throughout their body. This experience may indicate that the Lord intends to administer healing through you, or it may be the Lord's fiery presence manifesting as guidance, a witness, or a declaration of His delight in worship. While exhilarating, these experiences are simply a part of a much bigger whole.

The fire of God can be so glorious that it creates in us a desire for it to never end, as experienced by the two who walked with Jesus on the road to Emmaus. They were so engulfed in His presence and so fully absorbed by what He was revealing to them that they didn't want their experience with Him to end. Once their eyes were opened to realize it was Jesus, they proclaimed, "Why didn't we recognize him? Didn't our hearts burn with the flames of holy passion while we walked beside him?" (Luke 24:32). His presence is a fire that draws us in and fills us with passion.

On the opposite end of the spectrum, the fire of God can also have negative effects. This makes sense because fire has both positive and negative effects in the natural realm. We find warmth from a toasty blaze in a fireplace or a campfire in the cool of night, but if we touch the flames, our skin will be damaged. Likewise, if either of those fires extends beyond the designated placement, it brings destruction to whatever is in its path.

As I have pondered fire in Scripture, it seems to me to be twofold, bringing judgment and consumption. Fire brings judgment unto righteousness or unrighteousness and a consumption that brings either holy conviction or elimination.

Old Testament Fire

God manifested as a smoking pot and burning torch while making a covenant with Abraham in Genesis 15:17. The fire of God in this instance judged Abraham as righteous, and his heart was consumed with commitment to God.

In Exodus 3, God revealed Himself to Moses as a living flame of fire in a bush. The bush wasn't consumed, but Moses was. He was consumed with passion for the presence of God and fiery conviction to carry out the assignment God gave him.

Shadrach, Meshach, and Abednego were so consumed with love and honor for God that when they were thrown into the fiery furnace for not worshiping the king, the only things affected by the fire were the ropes that had bound them and those who threw them into the furnace.[1] In this story, we see these three men judged as righteous by the one who met them in the fire, delivering them from harm. Yet the same fire brought judgment against the unrighteousness of the king seeking worship for himself and against his servants who carried out his orders.

Leviticus tells how the people fell face down in worship when God came as fire from Heaven to consume their sacrifices presented to Him on the altar.[2] Yet in Genesis 19 and Numbers 11, when fire fell from Heaven, those who refused to repent for their unrighteous acts were consumed by a fiery judgment of condemnation.

New Testament Fire

The same God who came as fire in the Old Covenant comes as fire in the New Covenant. He "is always the same—yesterday, today, and forever" (Hebrews 13:8). Within the first three chapters of the New Testament, John the Baptist speaks of the fire of God's judgment. In Matthew 3:7, he rebuked the Pharisees: "You offspring of vipers! Who warned you to slither away like snakes from the fire of God's judgment?" He continues in verse 10, declaring, "Every fruitless, rotten tree will be chopped down and thrown into the fire." In verse 12, he tells how the wheat will be gathered into God's granary, but the straw will be burned up with "a fire that can't be extinguished."

Right in the middle of those verses above, John speaks of a fire connected to Holy Spirit that will be offered by the coming Messiah, telling them that those who repent (turn away from wicked ways and return to God's ways), "He will submerge you into union with the Spirit of Holiness and with a raging fire" (Matthew 3:11). It is those who choose to repent who are the wheat gathered into God's granary and those who refuse to repent are the straw. Both experience the fire of God but with different outcomes.

Baptism of Fire

Just before His ascension in Acts 1:5, Jesus told His disciples, "For John baptized you in water, but in a few days from now you will be baptized in the Holy Spirit!" He acknowledged John's baptism, the mark of repentance and a heart to follow God's ways, but then He introduced a baptism into the Spirit of Holiness with fire, just as John had prophesied at the river Jordan. Jesus prepared His disciples to be engulfed in the raging fire of the Holy Spirit.

Into union... These two words in Matthew 3:11 take us beyond our traditional understanding of baptism. Union implies living as one with the Spirit of Holiness and being continually submerged in His fire, causing an inundation that permeates our being.

Jesus had already given Holy Spirit to His disciples in John 20:22 by breathing on them and telling them to receive. This means that receiving Holy Spirit and being baptized in the Holy Spirit are different. Acts 2:1–4 tells how Holy Spirit came rushing and roaring as a violent wind out of the heavenly realm on the day of Pentecost, appearing as a pillar of fire that separated into tongues of fire that engulfed each one of the disciples who had been waiting as instructed. This passage is the basis of the common belief that the gift of tongues is the baptism of fire because all of them began to speak in languages unknown to them by the power of the Spirit. Merriam-Webster even references this passage in its second definition of baptism of fire.[3]

There is no denying the manifestation of the gift of tongues on the day of Pentecost. However, to limit our understanding to only that is a disservice to the Body of Christ because more happened in each of those disciples that day. They were seized with power just as Jesus said they would be: "But I promise you this—the Holy Spirit will come upon you, and you will be seized with power" (Acts 1:8).

The gift of tongues certainly endows us with power from Holy Spirit in numerous ways; two of which are the ability to pray the perfect will of God as He gives utterance and the building up of our most holy faith.[4] But more than a prayer language came to those men and women. They received something so powerful that it brought a divine shift in the depths of their being. They ceased hiding in fear and went forth, risking their lives to boldly proclaim the good news of Jesus Christ with words and demonstrations! They had been baptized with fire—immersed into the fire of God.

The phrase "baptism of fire" began to be used in 1625 to reference an introductory or initial experience that is a severe ordeal, such as a soldier's first exposure to enemy fire.[5] The disciples of the early church faced "enemy fire" in a way that the American church cannot comprehend. (However, many brothers and sisters in Christ from around the globe, who have experienced intense persecution, can certainly understand.) Because the disciples waited, they received this baptism of fire that both John the Baptist and Jesus prophesied would come. Submerged into union with the Spirit of Holiness, they were engulfed and consumed by the fiery presence of the Spirit of God. This fire seemed to burn off any fear they once had and remove hindrances that had kept them from walking in the resurrection life Jesus had given them.

Fiery Trials

While praying for more revelation and understanding of the fire of God for this chapter, a picture of Noah's Ark came to my mind's eye. God's promise to Noah about never again destroying the earth with a flood resounded in my spirit. It seemed strange that He would talk to me about the flood when I had asked for revelation about His fire.

There was such an emphasis on the word "flood." From the depths of my spirit came the thought: *He didn't say He wouldn't destroy the earth again...just not by a flood.* This led me to the question, "How would you do it, Lord?" He answered, "Fire." Perplexed, I asked, "Do you really plan to destroy the earth?" I waited and continued to ponder. Within moments, a thought bubbled up from my spirit: *What if He doesn't actually intend to destroy the earth as in the globe...but rather, our earth nature?*

Think this through with me, Genesis 8:21–22 tells of God's promise not to destroy the whole earth:

> And when Yahweh smelled the sweet fragrance of Noah's offerings his heart was stirred, and He said: "Never again will I curse the earth because of people, even though the imagination of their hearts are evil from their childhood; nor will I ever again destroy every living creature as I have done. I promise this: As long as earth exists there will always be seasons of planting and harvest, cold and heat, summer and winter, day and night."

And then He declared this promise:

> I establish my loving covenant with you, your descendants, and every living creature that is with you; animals large and small, birds, and every living thing that came out of the ark. I will maintain my loving covenant with you. I will never again completely destroy life on earth by means of a flood. Yes, never again will a flood destroy the whole earth!

— Genesis 9:9–11

God made a covenant with Noah and his descendants (that includes us) that He would never again destroy the whole earth, the globe, with a flood. He didn't say He wouldn't destroy part of the earth by another means, though, and technically, we are a part of the earth because we were fashioned and created from its dust. We inherited Adam's sin nature in our flesh, our individual pieces of earth. God could have wiped out all of humanity with the flood and started over, but instead, He saved Noah and his family. He had a desire and a plan for His image-bearers to conquer evil.

Peter speaks of the prophetic picture of the flood waters as a baptism, an immersion, that saves us.[6] The warning had been heralded, and only eight people boarded the ark, saved by obedience. The earth was cleansed of the overarching evil that had been embedded in those who refused to enter God's way of salvation. Yet the evil of our earth nature still had to be dealt with. God did not want to destroy mankind, so He made a way for us to overcome evil with good—Jesus.

When we are born again, our spirit becomes one with Holy Spirit, but we still have to work out our salvation in regard to the flesh. Jesus came to baptize us with His Spirit and fire to purge us of earth-natured tendencies. As He submerges us into union with the *raging fire of the Holy Spirit*, He burns away that which doesn't align with the Spirit of Holiness.

After the flood, God came as fire over and over again, and Peter chose to use the metaphor of fire when addressing challenges: "Beloved, do not be surprised at the fiery ordeal which is taking place to test you [that is, to test the quality of your faith], as though something strange or unusual were happening to you" (1 Peter 4:12 AMP). I can identify with whoever Peter was writing to because innumerable situations have caught me off guard. Peter made it clear: Our fiery trials are tests of our faith. All too often, I have failed to realize that my trials provide an opportunity to strengthen my faith and help me grow in maturity.

Refining Fire

Previously, I mentioned how fire can burn, damage, and destroy, but also provide light, warmth, and energy. Another aspect of fire is how it cleanses and purifies. A great example of how fire purifies is a metal refinery. Precious metals are placed inside a furnace and brought to extreme temperatures. The metals liquify, and impurities rise to the surface to be skimmed off repeatedly until the metal is pure. This is such a great picture of the work Jesus is doing in us. He purges us of the impurities of our earth nature, and He carefully watches over us throughout the refining process.

Who Is Jesus to You?

Malachi prophesied about Jesus as our Refiner:

Later, he further prophesied,

We tend to resist the fire that comes to refine us. Yet, Jesus is the refiner who purposes to burn away the wood, hay, and stubble of our lives—those things of our earth nature that have no eternal value. As we embrace our refining fire and yield to His purifying process, we become more and more free, and joy increases as treasures of the heavenly realm begin to emerge and shine radiantly from within us.

Salted by Fire

Jesus taught in Matthew 5:13 that our lives are like salt, and if we lose our saltiness, we become good for nothing and will be thrown out and trampled on by others. I used to think this meant we were a lost cause if we lost our saltiness, but that mindset goes against His mercy, redemption, and the finished work of the cross. I pondered this matter in my heart for several years, and one day, Holy Spirit connected the Scripture above to the following: "Everyone will pass through the fire and every sacrifice will be seasoned with salt" (Mark 9:49).

Jesus made it clear—everyone will pass through the fire. As we live our lives as living sacrifices, yielding to the fire in which we are submerged, we become seasoned with salt so that we can bring flavor to the world around us. If there are areas of our lives that lack flavor, chances are we will experience trials in that area to "salt" us.

The key is to embrace the fire and receive seasoning from our Lord Jesus. When we are salted by the fire, we also gain the ability to preserve peace in our union with one another.[7] Our fiery trials can be painful, but they bring life, purity, healing, joy, peace, and victory as impurities are removed.

We were created to have dominion in this world and reveal Jesus as we overcome. We are His modern-day Levites as the new song of praise to the Lamb declares, "You have chosen us to serve our God and formed us into a kingdom of priests who reign on the earth" (Revelation 5:10).

We have been chosen to serve God by reigning with Him. All that we experience is for our training. His fire comes to consume us with passion for Him and eliminate all that hinders us from being the pure vessels we have been fashioned and designed to be.

Jesus Is Our Fire

Jesus is the raging fire sent to baptize us, submerging us into union with His Spirit of Holiness. If our hearts are open to His name, His fire judges us as righteous, and He consumes us with passion to be like Him in nature and authority and continually immersed in His presence. If our hearts reject His name, the effects of His fire are quite different. The choice is ours.

The same words He spoke to the Shulamite in Song of Songs 8:6–7, He speaks to each of us:

> Fasten me upon your heart as a seal of fire forevermore. This living, consuming flame will seal you as my prisoner of love. My passion is stronger than the chains of death and the grave, all-consuming as the very flashes of fire from the burning heart of God. Place this fierce, unrelenting fire over your entire being. Rivers of pain and persecution will never extinguish this flame. Endless floods will be unable to quench this raging fire that burns within you. Everything will be consumed. It will stop at nothing as you yield everything to this furious fire until it won't even seem to you like a sacrifice anymore.

This is the baptism of fire. All that the Shulamite went through in her journey, letting go of the past and becoming what the Bridegroom King saw in her, was her refining process. He kept careful watch over her as she traversed the fire until she got to the place of total consumption and her surrendering was no longer a sacrifice.

She was salted in that fire as well. Her passionate pursuit of the Bridegroom King, despite the challenges she faced, piqued curiosity in those around her, and they began to search after Him for themselves.

Remember the young man I encountered at the service desk? He prayed that I would receive the baptism of fire. I didn't think anything happened that day, but I was wrong. Through the years, I have had a fervent passion for Jesus, for His righteousness, for His purpose, and His Kingdom, no matter the opinions of others.

Even in dark times, when I felt like giving up, when I got tangled and strangled by devastation, and during periods marked by turmoil, shortcomings, and failures, I persisted in pursuing Him. All the while, I was in the fire. Jesus didn't want me to continue as I was; His fire burned continually and faithfully, purging and purifying. Jesus held me in His hand, and He wouldn't let me go. I wouldn't let Him go either...I had been baptized in fire.

Jesus' love is intense, and He won't relent until we are completely consumed with fiery passion for Him. Thankfully, His refining process spans our lifetime here on earth. He knows the pace we can keep and the threshold of pain we can endure. We must simply yield. When the pain seems unbearable or situations bring uncertainty, we can press into Him and remember that only the ropes that bind us are devoured by the fire. We can trust Jesus to bring strength and the fire of His presence to walk with us, just as He did with the two on the road to Emmaus.

May we be like Moses, Shadrach, Meshach, and Abednego, and be people of righteousness who experience the fire of God in such a way that we are consumed with Him and judged righteous for honoring Him in all our ways. May we surrender to the baptism of fire—submerged into union with the Spirit of Holiness and engulfed in His raging fire. May we yield to our refining process and valiantly endure fiery trials as we are purified, seasoned, and transformed into the likeness of Jesus, *embracing and taking hold of* our Twofold Fire.

Points to Ponder

- The judgment of God in the life of a believer reveals His righteousness. Ponder a time He empowered you by revealing His work of righteousness in your life.
- Is there an aspect of your earth nature that you sense Holy Spirit is inviting you to yield to Him? Take a few minutes to surrender that portion of "earth" to His fire and ask Him what He has for you to receive instead.
- List some characteristics connected to your earth nature that the fire of the Lord has consumed and cleansed you from. Take a few moments to celebrate your victory in Jesus.

Prayer of Embrace

Thank you, Father, for Your master plan of sending Your Son to submerge me into union with the Spirit of Holiness and with a raging fire. Jesus, I yield my life and all my ambitions to You and invite You to continue burning away my earth nature. With every fiery trial I face, help me to embrace Your name, Your Fire, so that more of the precious gems You have planted within me may emerge. I receive the baptism of Holy Spirit that you sent to empower me to live the recreated life that Your sacrifice and resurrection purchased for me. Burn in me with holy passion until it doesn't even seem like a sacrifice anymore. Amen.

Prayer of the Refining Fire:

Jesus, another hurt has come to the surface. If I could have dealt with it, I would have, but I can't. Come and wipe away the dross, and remove the impurities that have risen from the depths of my soul. I invite Your blood to cleanse the areas of my heart that are now free from impurity. Thank You, Jesus. Holy Spirit, what do you want to fill the void with? (Take a few moments to listen, and then acknowledge and receive what you hear.) Thank You, Holy Spirit, I receive _____________ to fill the void and plead the blood of Jesus to seal this divine exchange. Amen.

Part Three

Embrace

Our Sacred Response

Chapter 19

Heavenly Captor

Ah, Lord God, thou holy lover of my soul,
when thou comest into my heart,
all that is within me shall rejoice.
—Thomas à Kempis, *Of the Imitation of Christ* —

For you reach into my heart. With one flash of your eyes
I am undone by your love, my beloved, my equal, my bride.
You leave me breathless—I am overcome by merely a glance
from your worshiping eyes, for you have stolen my heart.
I am held hostage by your love and by the graces
of righteousness shining upon you.
—Song of Songs 4:9—

ALL OF US ARE CAPTIVE TO SOMETHING, ALTHOUGH MOST OF US
wouldn't consider ourselves in bondage because the chains that hold
us are invisible. We tend to be so accustomed to those invisible chains
that we aren't even aware we are in captivity. Many of us in the Body
of Christ are not experiencing the depths of the intimate love rela-

tionship with God that we were fashioned for because our souls have been captured by the distractions of the natural realm.

Whatever the specific distractions may be, anything hindering our hearts from being captivated by the passionate love of Jesus is a chain that binds us. Let's explore what it is (or looks like) to embrace Jesus, our Heavenly Captor, the true lover of our soul.

In Exodus, we see the Israelites, God's chosen people, living in bondage in the very place they had gone for refuge from famine. Egypt wasn't the land promised to the Israelites; it was meant to be a temporary residence, a place of reprieve. What was intended as a blessing became a curse. Why? Why did God allow Pharaoh to enslave His people?

Maybe their hearts were captivated by the rich lands and abundant harvests instead of the One who provided them. Maybe they thought that Egypt was the source of their bounty instead of what it really was—the mark of God's favor and blessing upon His chosen people. Maybe the Egyptian world system or their false gods had captured their devotion away from God.

Whatever the reason, they neglected the original directive God had given Abraham, Isaac, and Jacob. While God had caused them to prosper in that foreign nation, His intent and purpose was to make them a nation of their own. Eventually, out of fear that the Israelites would rise up and overpower Egypt, Pharaoh enslaved them. What a picture of how the enemy oppresses us. He is so fearful of God's people that he schemes to keep us in bondage in hopes of keeping us from taking hold of God's plan for our lives.

After four hundred years of bondage, God sent Moses, the promised deliverer, to rescue the Israelites from captivity. In leading them out, God desired to captivate their heart and bring them into an intimate relationship of covenantal love. However, except for a few people out of hundreds of thousands, it seems the people of Israel could not comprehend the intimacy of the covenant God made with them. The bondage of Egypt remained in their hearts even after God provided a way out.

Both Ends of the Spectrum—Love Empowers, Evil Controls

The definition of "captive" tends to bring a negative connotation and understandably so, as it means one taken and held in confinement, dominated, or controlled.[1] The word "captor" is understood to be one who has captured a person or thing,[2] and it doesn't typically create a positive image either. According to our understanding of this natural world, no one in their right mind would choose to be a captive, nor would they want to be dominated and controlled by another person. So why would I highlight Captor as one of Jesus' names and encourage you to be captive to Him? Because on every spectrum, there are two ends.

On one end of the spectrum, there are captors with evil intentions. Holding people in bondage against their will, these captors are abusive and bring harm or death for selfish gain. There are many examples of them throughout history: tyrants like Pharaoh, Genghis Khan, and Hitler, to name a few. In our modern world, there are tyrants who lead countries, terrorist groups, human trafficking rings, and many other types of groups that inflict devastating harm on those under their control.

On the other end of the spectrum are those who capture people with extreme kindness, generosity, and love. Maybe you've heard the statement, "He has captivated my heart." Jesus is above all others in this category. He doesn't captivate by force, domination, manipulation, or control. In fact, being captivated is quite the opposite of being a captive. To be captivated by Jesus is to find Him irresistible and become captured by His traits, the nature and character of who He is. Jesus is a captor with the purest intention, and He captivates us by lavishing His love upon us and drawing us deeper into His heart.

The Lover of Our Soul

Jesus is the ultimate lover of our soul. He invites us to rest in His luxurious love.[3] He is not the type of captor who incites the fear of punishment, abuse, or torture. Rather, Jesus lavishes us with His love in such a way as to captivate us and draw us to Himself so we can receive the goodness He has for us.

Ephesians 4:8 reveals Jesus as our Heavenly Captor: "When He ascended on high, He led captivity captive" (AMP). I have read this many times through the years and have wondered, "What does it mean to lead captivity captive?" In the Passion Translation, the same verse reads, "He ascends into the heavenly heights taking his many captured ones with Him." My understanding began to blossom as I pondered this translation, connecting it to the fact that we are now co-seated with Christ in the heavenly realm.[4] Jesus broke the barrier between Heaven and earth, and our spirits are already seated with Him in victory. But not just anyone...His "captured" ones.

The psalmist prophesied this amazing truth centuries before in Psalm 68:18: "He ascends into the heavenly heights, taking his many captured ones with Him, leading them in triumphal procession." *Taking His many captured ones.* For Jesus to have "many captured ones" makes "captor" an essence of who He is. He longs to capture our soul, which is the *essence of who we are.* This capturing isn't by force, though. He won't use His authority against our free will. He does, however, intend to captivate us with His love. Has He captured you?

It is important to note that following rules doesn't equate to love. And following rules doesn't cultivate intimacy. If following rules equated to love for God, then the Pharisees wouldn't have been rebuked by

Jesus. Rather, they would've been applauded because they followed rules explicitly. Instead, Jesus esteemed the lowly who had experienced His merciful forgiveness and reciprocated His love in humble worship.

When a person is overcome by the goodness, generosity, tender care, and concern of another, deep gratitude and love are cultivated. Love reciprocates. When a person comes to the place of realizing the depth of love Jesus poured out at Calvary and continues to pour out, they open their hearts and are compelled to love Him in return.

Old Testament Examples of People Captivated by the Love of God

There are many examples of people captivated by the love of God throughout the Old Testament. These people, such as Noah, Abraham, Moses, and David, *knew* God intimately and responded with such devotion, even without the indwelling of Holy Spirit.

David stands out as one who surpassed most people in his understanding of the love of God. It is clear through his psalms and the story of his life that he knew God intimately. He was willing to put himself in harm's way as a teen as he faced Goliath and be "undignified" in his worship, even as a noble king, because of his passionate love for God and for the honor of His Name.

New Testament Examples of Being Captivated by Jesus

The early church was full of people who had been captivated by Jesus, beginning with the twelve disciples. There was something about Jesus that touched them in such a way that they were willing to leave life as usual to follow Him. When others turned back, not fully understanding all He was saying and doing, they stayed. When faced with severe persecution, they were so captivated by Jesus that they became martyrs, willing to lay down their lives for Him, just as He had for them.

Mary, the sister of Lazarus, was a captive of Jesus. She is known for sitting at Jesus' feet alongside the men while He taught. John 12:3 tells how "Mary picked up an alabaster jar filled with nearly a liter of extremely rare and costly perfume—the purest extract of nard, and she anointed Jesus' feet. Then she wiped them dry with her long hair." Jesus delighted in her expression of love.

Paul, like Mary, lived in extreme devotion to Jesus. After his encounter with revelation-light on the road to Damascus, he went from vehemently hating and killing Jesus' followers to becoming a passionate follower himself. Jesus wasn't physically forcing him or manipulating him to do anything, yet Paul considered himself a *prisoner* of the Lord.[5] It is easy to surrender yourself to someone who loves you so deeply, regardless of the many reasons not to do so. Paul lived in the reality that has been gifted to every follower of Jesus: "Every spiritual blessing in the heavenly realm has already been lavished upon us as a love gift" (Ephesians 1:3). He was captivated, and Jesus was his captor.

Distractions

Regardless of the era, whether Old or New Testament or our current day, we all face distractions that hinder our intimacy with Jesus. It is easy to be captivated by the wrong thing. The Israelites provide an example of how susceptible humans are to distractions. They were miraculously delivered from their oppressor by the power of God, yet remained in bondage within their heart. It seems they were captivated by His miracles rather than by His love for them.

Saul, King David's predecessor, got caught up in seeking the acceptance of the people and doing things in his own strength. The Pharisees were distracted by the world system with its hunger for power and prestige. While Mary was unmoved by those around her as she anointed Jesus and wept at His feet, her spectators were distracted by her past and by her extravagant devotion. Even Jesus' siblings were distracted, and they didn't believe He was the Messiah until after His resurrection. Perhaps public opinions, local gossip, or envy diverted their attention.

What distracts us? It takes courage to consider what may be distracting our hearts from being completely captivated by our heavenly captor, the lover of our soul. We can be captive to a myriad of things, such as people, expectations, thoughts, habits, and lifestyles. Our hobbies and recreation, money and material possessions, and desire to be important and known can create interference. We can be diverted by numerous fears and insecurities, the pain and sorrow we carry, grief and weariness, and habitual sin. Good things like our goals, successes, accomplishments, and even our family can become an obstruction to our devotion to Jesus.

The culture we're a part of, along with all the opinions circulating on news networks and social media platforms, provides a host of distractions as well. Probably one of the most sneaky and undetected captivities for Christians is religion. A religious mindset thinks that following rules and rituals brings us close to God and believes that if we're good enough, we will receive some blessings and one day enter Heaven.

Religion limits our ability to surrender to the grace and lavishing love of our heavenly captor because it focuses on the external and causes us to think we must *do* in order to *earn* His love. With a religious mindset, a person is often distracted by a list of to-dos, rules, and procedures to follow to be acceptable to God. However, the truth is, we don't have to earn His love; we simply need to receive it.

The distractions that hold us captive don't do so by force, but rather by deception or ignorance. Most aren't evil or bad, yet they hold us in bondage just the same—knowingly or unknowingly.

Another distraction to be on guard against is being captivated only by what God does *for* us. As the lover of our soul, Jesus loves us for who we are—the unique individual He made us to be—and He longs for us to love Him for *who He is*. He desires an intimate love relationship with each of us. In loving relationships, each person cares for and gives to the other from the depth of love shared. Goodness overflows from one to the other. Out of His love for us, Jesus laid down His life, giving us all He had to give. As His captured ones, we give back to Him from the overflow of love. When we open our hearts to be captivated by His love, nothing can separate us from it.

Becoming His Shulamite—Lavished in His Love

"Captor" and "lover" must go hand-in-hand because love, in its purest form, is captivating. God is love, and the love that God gives is the love that Jesus gives. He doesn't love like the world loves. As our lover, He is not looking to seduce us for selfish desires, and He doesn't manipulate us with a sense of obligation.

Jesus, as our lover, tenderly cares for our hearts. He gently nurtures us into wholeness. He carries our wounded soul for as long as it takes to bring us back to health. He lifts us out of the miry clay of all the distractions of life that we've been stuck in. He takes us from the captivity of religion—rituals and rules without an intimate relationship—into freedom and liberty within the very heart of God. It is in this freedom that we are truly captivated—captive to His nature, captive to His goodness, captive to His glory. To be separate from Him is unacceptable, so we willingly become captive to the greatest lover our soul could ever know.

The Shulamite in the Song of Songs is a noteworthy example of being captivated by the lavishing love of God. Her story is an example of the process all of God's people must go through. We see her struggle with the issues of life as she longs to experience the depths of the love of the Bridegroom. She is so captivated by His love that she presses on through the transformation process, overcoming unbelief concerning her worth and the challenges of her past and present, releasing the pains of life, and grabbing hold of her true identity. She even had to press past the obligations of religion.[6]

Her beloved (Jesus) only sees her through eyes of love, finding delight in her regardless of her weakness. As she identifies her sense of unworthiness and the areas in her life that are dark and undesirable, He only speaks of the redemption He has provided. He tells her of her beauty and strength, how she ravishes His heart, and the sweet fragrance that comes from the garden He is cultivating within her. She, like us, had mountains that stood between her and the Bridegroom, challenges that kept her from believing she could overcome them. But He called her higher and beckoned her to come and run upon the mountaintops with Him.

Despite the setbacks, the Shulamite continued to pursue the Bridegroom King because He had captured her heart. He saw what she was becoming, and as soon as she fully accepted His view and the value He placed in her, she set her gaze on Him alone and was transported into His glorious embrace. She became His prisoner of love, caught up with Him in His cloud-filled chamber, overcome by His lavishing love.

Relentless Pursuit of Freedom

Many in the Body of Christ, like the Israelites, consistently struggle with distractions that hinder them from keeping Jesus as their focus. May we be like the Shulamite and overcome every distraction by relentlessly pursuing our Bridegroom King as we lay down the pains of this life. May we rid ourselves of the mindsets that hold us captive to the earthly realm and overthrow the snare of religion that hinders intimate relationship with Him. May we be captivated by His ceaseless, extravagant love and join the company of captured ones living from the heavenly realm with all heavenly blessing, where Jesus has already led us.

Living as His captive is living in true freedom. As His captives, we are free to be who He created us to be: His son, His daughter, His image-bearer and glory carrier. As His captives, we are free to live and function according to His design and purpose for our lives, not because we are forced, but from the overflow of love and joy.

As captives of Jesus, we are free to love from the reality of His Kingdom on earth as it is in Heaven because the heavenly realm is our reality. No longer are we captive to what was; our past does not define us or determine our future. We are free from sin, free from old habits and mindsets. As His captives, we have been made holy and are free to live according to His holiness and righteousness. Not only are we in His Kingdom, but His Kingdom is in us![7]

Jesus truly is the lover of our soul. Because of His profound love for us, He gave His all when He chose Calvary. From this same love comes the freedom we have been given to choose whether we reciprocate it or not. It's as if I hear Him saying, "I did all this for you because I love you; I want you to choose Me because of your love for Me." He longs for hearts that have been captivated by His love.

The Israelites longed for freedom from their bondage in Egypt but were seemingly unaware of the captivity that held their souls. After only knowing suffering, they struggled to comprehend intimacy with the One who freed them. It seems that the Israelites were frightened by God's fiery presence as they stood before Him at Mt. Sinai. They were unfamiliar with the concept of a loving God seeking to have connection with them through covenant.

The conditions and boundaries of God's covenant may have seemed like a list of demands, reminding them of their bondage in Egypt. Their life experience was the lens through which they were looking. They were so used to being under an abusive leader who controlled and manipulated them for selfish gain. Maybe they likened God to Pharaoh and feared opening their heart to a personal relationship with Him.

As Moses relayed what God was saying to the Israelites, they may have misunderstood the boundaries being set. Perhaps they saw them as control instead of protection, not understanding that God's intention for them was good. I wonder how many people can relate to this. The pains of life on earth can be so overwhelming. The people who are supposed to love and protect us so often are the ones who hurt us the most due to their own pain and dysfunction. This makes it challenging to believe that a relationship with God will be any different.

If we search for freedom outside of God, we become captive to things, people, beliefs, and mindsets that are empty and false. For this reason, Jesus came to "bring good news to the humble and afflicted; to bind up [the wounds of] the brokenhearted, to proclaim release [from confinement and condemnation] to the [physical and spiritual] captives and freedom to prisoners" (Isaiah 61:1 AMP). Upon completing His mission on earth and the cross, Jesus then "led captivity captive" (Ephesians 4:8 AMP), "ascending into the heavenly heights taking his many captured ones with Him" (Ephesians 4:8 TPT).

He has done the work to release us from every bondage. He has opened the prison doors to set us free. Let's be like Noah, Moses, Abraham, and David, who grabbed hold of God instead of being prisoners to their circumstances and failures. Let's be like the disciples who walked with Jesus and keep following Him no matter the cost, even when life is painful, and His way doesn't make sense.

Let's be like Mary and reciprocate Jesus' lavishing love, expending our best and most costly offerings at His feet in worship. Let's be like Paul and allow the transformational love of Jesus to overpower all we thought we knew. Let's become like the Shulamite and simply fall in love with Jesus, allowing Him to be the captor of our hearts. May we let go of ourselves and follow Him as He leads us upon the mountaintops. Let's seek Jesus above all other people and things, recognizing and forsaking distractions that aim to hinder our intimacy with Him.

We can be confident in the reality that Jesus is the lover of our soul and that He tenderly cares for us from the goodness of His nature and character. He loves us more than we can think or comprehend. As we surrender ourselves to His lavishing love, we become captivated by the depth of that love and His undying devotion to complete His work in us.

The more love we receive, the more we open our hearts to being captured into deeper intimacy with Jesus. By living in deeper intimacy, we can view our lives from our position in the heavenly realm, and distractions begin to lose their hold on us. All of this takes place as we *take hold of His name* and *embrace* Jesus as our Heavenly Captor.

Points to Ponder

- Are you able to identify with the Israelites in their struggle to trust God? In what way?
- What distractions did Holy Spirit highlight for you that He wants to help you eliminate? Ask Him for divine strategy and Scripture to wield.
- In what way can you identify with the Shulamite in the Song of Songs? How has Jesus captivated your heart so far?

Prayer of Embrace

Jesus, thank You for setting me free from the bondage of this earthly realm. Thank You for being the lover of my soul and lavishing me with Your love, for seeing me through Your eyes of redemption. Help me to identify the distractions keeping me from entering deeper intimacy with You and to remove them from my life. I desire to give You my deepest devotion, and I want to be captivated by who You are, not what You do for me. Help me to live from my place with You in the heavenly realm as I follow You in my daily life. I surrender myself to You as my heavenly Captor. Amen.

Chapter 20

Unshakable Foundation

The loftier the building,
the deeper must the foundation be laid.
—Thomas à Kempis, *The Imitation of Christ*—

His eyes of faith were set on the city
with unshakable foundations,
whose architect and builder is God himself.
—Hebrews 11:10—

IN THE REALM OF CONSTRUCTING BUILDINGS, THE FOUNDATION of a structure affects its strength, quality, safety, and longevity. Even the most lavish structures are only as good as the foundation they are built on. The same is true for our lives. With all the promises in the Word of God that tell of the favor and blessing God intends for His children, it is a wonder why many experience instability and lack in various areas of life.

While there is not one explanation that fits all, there is one factor that applies to all: whether we build our lives on a shakable or unshakable foundation. If the ground isn't solid, the structure will fail... eventually.

In 1913, the Transcona Grain Elevator was built near Winnipeg, Manitoba, Canada. Its foundation was formed with a massive concrete slab on clay soil. The first thin layer of clay was soft but beneath it was "relatively stiff clay."[1] Once the construction was completed and the tanks were filled not quite to capacity, large settlements of the storage building were noticed. Within one hour, there was a significant tilt, and within twenty-four hours, the foundation soil collapsed, causing the structure to tilt about 27°.

Because other buildings in the area were built on this clay, it was assumed, with the knowledge they had at the time, that the soil would uphold the grain elevator. Even with such a large concrete base, the weight of the grain revealed the lack of strength in the foundation beneath it. As Christians, we could equate our faith in Jesus to the massive concrete foundation of the Transcona Grain Elevator and think that He simply covers the imperfect "soil" in our hearts. However, Jesus isn't a slab we lay on top of our current foundation. He must *be* the foundation.

Our Clay Foundation

As I covered in "Redeemer," Adam's choice to disobey God brought evil into the existence of humanity. His action is commonly known as "the fall." God's design was for each of us to be founded on, live in, and radiate His glory; but because Adam and Eve fell, we all fall short of God's glory.[2] However, there is good news!

Ephesians 1:4 tells us, "And in love He chose us before He laid the foundation of the universe." What a powerful truth! We could soak in the reality and encouragement of those words for a while. But there is more I want to share with you.

Until writing this, I only understood "before He laid the foundation of the universe" to mean before God fashioned the earth. However, the footnote for this verse in The Passion Translation reveals a truth that takes us further: "The word for 'fall' (Adam's fall) is kataboles, which can mean 'falling down,' but is usually translated as 'foundation' (of the world)."[3] The deeper meaning is that Adam's fall or "falling down" is the "foundation" of the earthly realm. As sad as that is, if we apply this deeper meaning to Ephesians 1:4, we see plainly that we were known, loved, and chosen by God before Adam ever fell!

Unfortunately, because Adam did fall, every human is born upon the clay foundation of a fallen nature. Fallen from what? Perfect union with our creator and His glory. Adam's choice of disobedience is our foundation until we choose a different one. The only other option is to be restored to the foundation God established before Adam fell: Jesus.

Foundation of All Things

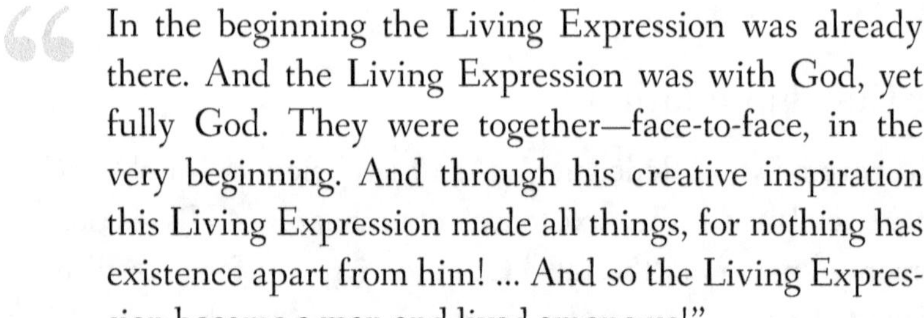

> In the beginning the Living Expression was already there. And the Living Expression was with God, yet fully God. They were together—face-to-face, in the very beginning. And through his creative inspiration this Living Expression made all things, for nothing has existence apart from him! ... And so the Living Expression became a man and lived among us!"
>
> — John 1:1–3, 14

Jesus is the very foundation upon which everything was created. "For in him was created the universe of things, both in the heavenly realm and on the earth, all that is seen and all that is unseen...He existed before anything was made, and now everything finds completion in him" (Colossians 1:16–17).

The foundation of creation was and is the Spirit of the Living God. Before anything was—He was. Before anything existed—He existed. Jesus is God, and He is the *very* Word that went forth in the beginning and created what was spoken. From Him, everything that exists was made. We are a part of the "all things" that were created through Him and for Him. And in Him, we are held together. He desires to be the foundation in every facet of our existence, but He leaves the choice to us.

It isn't difficult for me to think of Jesus as the foundation of all that is visible. However, it takes intentional consideration to determine if Jesus is the foundation of the thoughts and beliefs in my heart. There are many voices, thoughts, and opinions in this world that influence how we perceive and believe.

As believers in Jesus Christ, our faith must be founded on Jesus and His Word. Any teaching, cultural norm, or personal belief that does not align with the Word of God must not be one that we align with. When Jesus is the foundation of our lives, everything is determined by Him. Our thoughts, words, behaviors, responses, reactions, beliefs, and convictions will all be rooted in Jesus. He is our filter and the lens through which we view our situations and the world around us. As our foundation, He becomes the starting point of all our processes.

Jesus, Our Cornerstone

The prophet Isaiah speaks of our sure foundation in Isaiah 28:16: "Here's what the Lord God says: 'Behold, I set in place in Zion a Foundation Stone, fully tested and proven to be faithful and secure. And written upon this precious cornerstone is this: "Those who trust in him will not act in haste."' David spoke of this cornerstone a few hundred years prior: "The very stone the masons rejected as flawed has turned out to be the most important capstone of the arch, holding up the very house of God" (Psalm 118:22).

Peter, filled with the Holy Spirit, spoke to the elders and rulers of the people in Acts 4:11, saying, "This Jesus is the 'stone that you, the builders, have rejected, and now He has become the cornerstone.'" And Paul declared, "For no one is empowered to lay an alternative foundation other than the good foundation that exists, which is Jesus Christ!" (1 Corinthians 3:11).

All these Scriptures speak of Jesus as our cornerstone and of the reality that not everyone accepts Him as such. Ancient cornerstones were the first stones set in the foundation of a building and would often determine measurements and guide the workers in their course. Typically, the cornerstone was the largest, and every other stone was placed in alignment with it. Jesus, then, as our cornerstone, is who we must be in alignment with.

Jesus, Our Stonemason

Did you know that Jesus probably wasn't a woodworking carpenter? The Greek word *tekton*, often translated as carpenter, is more accurately rendered "craftsman" or "builder." Without considering the Jewish cultural background, a carpenter could fit that description. However, because trees were and still are rather scarce in the northern region of Israel where Jesus lived, making a living as a carpenter would have been challenging at best. In fact, the majority of homes in Israel were made of stone.[4]

Ponder the probability that the well-meaning translator, when choosing the word carpenter for Jesus' occupation, understood it to include the work of a stonemason. If we allow ourselves to accept this, immediately, so many Scriptures become more poignant, such as the Scriptures previously mentioned.

With this in mind, let's consider how Jesus Himself spoke about the need for a strong foundation when he shared the following parable in Matthew 7:24–27:

> Everyone who hears my teaching and applies it to his life can be compared to a wise man who built his house on an unshakable foundation. When the rains fell and the flood came, with fierce winds beating upon his house, it stood firm because of its strong foundation. But everyone who hears my teaching and does not apply it to his life can be compared to a foolish man who built his house on sand. When it rained and rained and the flood came, with wind and waves beating upon his house, it collapsed and was swept away.

This parable is a vivid picture, and it concluded a thorough teaching full of instructions, warnings, and examples as to how to live. Jesus gave imagery to help His hearers understand and to communicate His truths across languages, cultures, and time. He was clear and concise. He spoke with bold courage, power, and authority. He ended this teaching by clearly communicating that hearing wasn't enough. Rather, it is *applying* His teaching to our lives—actually living it out—that makes us wise and places us upon a strong, rock-solid, *unshakable foundation*.

As a stonemason, Jesus understood the importance of a sure foundation and used His knowledge to paint a picture of how vital His teachings are. God's truth, His Word, creates the foundation that enables us to withstand the storms of life, to stand firm through all our situations and circumstances.

A strong, unshakable foundation is a definite contrast to sand. Sand shifts and moves with pressure. By simply stepping upon a beach, we can see that even the smallest weight moves the sand beneath it—not to mention the rains, winds, and mighty waves that crash upon the shore during a storm.

Jesus declared that those who chose not to apply His teachings were like a foolish man. Thus, when the storms of life came, difficulties and troubles would get the best of them, and they would collapse and be swept away. Adam provides an illustration of this for us; he listened to God's instructions, but he didn't apply them when he faced temptation.

Limitations of Clay

Think of the soft clay that was under the Transcona Grain Elevator. Much like the clay foundation we inherited from Adam, it couldn't uphold the weight placed upon it. I have experienced a sort of tilting like that elevator in my personal life (more than once), which I have referred to in previous chapters. Due to unhealed areas in my soul, there were faulty areas of foundation in the soil of my heart. Therefore, during difficult times, I struggled with the weight of life and circumstances.

The struggle was perplexing for me because I had somehow developed a false belief that there would be fewer troubles in life after I became born again. I had fallen fervently in love with Jesus and was consumed with passion and hunger for Him. He was the *rock* of my salvation. When I read His Word, I took it to mean what it said and began living accordingly. Unfortunately, over time, without me realizing it, things in my life began to tilt. It was so subtle.

Before I recognized what was happening, my passion for Jesus turned into "works" for acceptance. My subtle transition from fervent love into works was devastating and damaging in many ways. I hadn't realized that becoming born again was only the beginning of building my life upon Jesus as my rock-solid foundation. Nor did I understand that much like the Transcona Grain

Elevator, the soil beneath the "concrete slab" of Jesus was wreaking havoc.

The foundation of my faith was indeed Jesus Christ; I *knew* Him as God and Savior. However, there were large areas of my inner world crumbling due to my clay foundation and underlying sand. I had to discover and face the areas in my life where false belief systems and carnal mindsets were still ruling.

With so much swirling within me, I threw my hands in the air and said, "Here you go, God. Here is everything I've learned and have been taught about You. I need You to teach me by Your Spirit and by Your Word. I. Need. YOU!"

It was many years ago that I came to this pivotal point in my faith walk. Since then, I have come to understand that surrendering our lives to Jesus is the starting point of establishing Him as our foundation. We each have a personal responsibility to rebuild every aspect of our lives in alignment with Him as the chief cornerstone, removing clay and sand along the way.

The engineers of the Transcona Grain Elevator were able to save the structure by rebuilding a proper foundation under it. It was a process of investigating what was there and learning what was needed. The same is true of us. With open hearts, we can hear Holy Spirit as He highlights faulty areas in the foundations of our lives that need to be replaced. As we listen and apply Jesus' teachings, we deconstruct the clay foundation and build on Him.

Bringing Everything into Alignment

Building our life on Jesus as our foundation starts with faith— embracing the essence of who He is. However, faith is only one of many aspects that our lives are comprised of. Scripture is full of teachings that address every area of life. The following are some aspects of our lives that Jesus specifically addressed in Matthew 5–7, the Sermon on the Mount, that need to be founded on His teaching, His Word.

Our Character – Are we humble, meek, gentle, and merciful toward others? Do we crave righteousness? Is our heart pure and pursuing peace? Are our motives pure? Do we appreciate people for who they are or only value them for what we can gain from them? Are we willing to be anonymous in our good deeds? Do we care more about the things of earth—this world system—than the things of God's Kingdom? Is our money a tool, or do we worship it? Do we value earthly treasures above God?

Our Thoughts – Do we lust after things or people that are not ours? Do we think negatively of others or ourselves? Is the cup always half empty, or do we choose to release hope by speaking the reality of God's Kingdom into situations? Are we full of worry, or are we trusting our Father in Heaven? Do we judge others yet neglect to examine our own hearts?

Our Trust – Are we fully dependent on God and willing to wait on Him? Do we entrust our life to the one who gave it to us? Are we allowing fear of the unknown or the fear of man to overrule our trust in God? Do we trust we will be rewarded for our obedience in this life and the life to come? Are we asking, seeking, and knocking with the expectation of the good He has in store for us?

Our Words – How do we speak to and about others and ourselves? Do our words point to Jesus? Do our words encourage and bring hope? Do we keep our word and promises? Are we degrading others with sarcasm, manipulation, or coercion to get our way? Do we speak words of honor and respect?

Our Actions – Do we treat people the way we want to be treated? Are we following Jesus' example of serving others and being helpful? Do we seek attention or approval with our behaviors? Do we make choices that bring harm, or do we seek to bless and build up in all we do?

Our Relationships – Do we forgive those who have hurt us? Are we faithful to our spouse, children, and friends? Do we choose to be loving to our enemies? Who do we align with—whether individuals, organizations, or movements—and do they align with the character of God? Do our relationships produce the fruit of righteousness?

All these areas of our lives must be founded upon and in alignment with Jesus, our cornerstone, or we will be unstable and experience tumultuous consequences when the storms of life come. Although we experience discomfort, He will often use the storms that come our way to wash away all that isn't in alignment with Him. All the while, Jesus keeps us safe and secure as we cling to the Rock. We can trust that the foundation He provides is superior.

Jesus declared in Matthew 5:3–9 that we are blessed, enriched, happy, fortunate, delightful, blissful, and content when our inner man is founded on His character, the essence of who He is.[5] From the foundation of faith in Jesus as God and Savior, His character is deposited within us by Holy Spirit in seed form and is developed as we become like Him. Our outer lives reflect the transformation of the inner man.

The words of Jesus in Matthew 7:24, "Everyone who hears my teaching and applies it to his life can be compared to a wise man who built his house on an unshakable foundation," is not a one-and-done type of application. Our initial decision to commit our lives to Jesus is only the beginning. Building upon Jesus as the foundation of our lives is a process. Thankfully, we aren't in this process alone.

As we continue life with Jesus, He is faithful to teach us. He will highlight areas of our lives that have sandy foundations. He will walk us through the deconstruction of our old ways and help us rebuild, established on His Word. Often, He will highlight specific Scriptures to pray and declare over ourselves and our situations to establish Him as the foundation in that area. His Word becomes our reality as we diligently speak what He has spoken.

Ultimately, each of us is responsible for the foundation we choose to build our life on. If we choose not to apply His Word, Jesus honors our choice, but He isn't responsible for the consequences of that choice. I am confident that when I "threw" all my knowledge of God in the air years ago and asked Him to teach me, it was by the unction of Holy Spirit. Since then, He has been bringing me into alignment with the head cornerstone.

Our lives are the "houses" we are building, and the strength and quality of our houses are determined by the foundation we build on. As our foundation, Jesus is our source of life and stability. By applying Jesus' teachings, the weak and unstable matter in the soil of our hearts and souls—the foundation we inherited from Adam—is replaced with the reality of God's Kingdom realm. By obeying, trusting, and partnering with His Word, we are wise builders, *embracing and taking hold of* Jesus as our Unshakable Foundation.

Points to Ponder

- Are you empowered to know that you were loved and chosen before Adam fell? How does the meaning of foundation in Ephesians 1:4 impact you?
- Invite Holy Spirit to reveal any aspect of your life that is still experiencing the effects of the clay foundation you inherited from Adam. What is it?
- Ask Jesus to reveal His living Word regarding the area identified above. What Scripture came to mind? Speak this

truth until it is secure as part of your unshakeable foundation.

Prayer of Embrace

Jesus, I accept that You are the foundation I must build every area of my life upon. Help me to identify and deconstruct any area that is still founded on the clay foundation of this earth realm. As I yield to You and apply the rock-solid truths of Your Word, replace every faulty, weak, and insufficient area with the reality of who You are. I embrace and take hold of You, Jesus, as my unshakable foundation. Amen.

Chapter 21

Embrace His Name

Unless the church is equipping believers to embrace
the values and vision of the kingdom of God and turn
away from the materialism, consumerism, greed,
and power of the present age, it not only abandons its
biblical mandate, it is rendered missionally ineffective.
—Alan Hirsch, *The Faith of Leap*—

For those of us who desire to follow Jesus, here is the
reality we must turn and face: If we're not being
intentionally formed by Jesus himself, then it's highly likely
we are being unintentionally formed by someone or
something else.
—John Mark Comer, *Practicing the Way*—

Be transformed as you embrace the glorious Christ-within
as your new life and live in union with him! For God has
re-created you all over again in his perfect righteousness,
and you now belong to him in the realm of true holiness.
—Ephesians 4:24—

WE STARTED OUR EXPLORATION INTO THE NAME OF JESUS WITH this Scripture: "But those who embraced him [Jesus] and took hold of his name he gave authority to become the children of God!" (John 1:12). I've repeated the words "embrace and take hold of" throughout each chapter to emphasize that receiving and believing in Jesus demands a response of grabbing hold of the character and authority of Jesus. Those words break down misconceptions and make it clear that it is only in knowing the essence of Jesus and all that His name encompasses that we are given the authority to become children of God.

John the Baptist warned the religious leaders who came to listen to him at the river, "Even when he [Messiah] stands among you, you will not recognize or *embrace* him!" (John 1:26, emphasis added). They *knew about* Yahweh, but they didn't *know* Him; therefore, both John and Jesus rebuked them over and over. We don't want to be like them. We must guard our hearts and hold onto Jesus. May we never get to the place of thinking we have experienced all of God or know everything there is to know about Him. He is unfathomable, and we will spend eternity exploring the fullness of who He is.

Mandate of the Ages

The requirement to *embrace and take hold of* God isn't new; it was the same mandate established in the Old Testament. God created us for a reciprocal relationship with Him, and He only expects *from* us what He is willing to do or has already done *for* us. He embraced all of humanity as He embraced the dust of the earth to shape and form Adam. Adam functioned in and from the character and essence of God until he disobeyed and stepped outside of God's embrace.

God embraced the Israelites by leading them out of Egypt and revealing His fiery devotion at Mt. Sinai. They were invited to take hold of Yahweh by entering into a covenant with Him. It's the same for us, only we have been invited into a new and better covenant through the person and blood of Jesus. When we say yes to Him, we enter a divine embrace with His name.

Every human is presented with a crossroads. John the Baptist's call to "keep turning away from evil and turn back to God" in Matthew 3:2 brought awareness to the crossroads we all face. His message reflected that of Jeremiah's: "Yahweh said to his people: 'Stand at the crossroads. Now, consider your ways and ask for the ancient paths. Which is God's way? Walk on his path, and you'll enjoy a resting place for yourselves'" (Jeremiah 6:16).

For Jeremiah's audience, to return to the ancient path was to return to the Torah, the books written by Moses. In those books were the recorded words of Yahweh—the instructions for living in covenant with I AM. In the last book of the Torah, the law is reviewed, and instruction is given. They were to destroy the altars of false gods in the land they were dispossessing, burn the Asherah poles in the fire, wipe out the names of the false gods, and not worship Yahweh according to the customs of other nations. These demands were all for the purpose of keeping them on the ancient path so there would be a place for Yahweh's name to dwell.[1]

A Place to Dwell

From the beginning, God has been seeking a place for His name to dwell, and He still is. Jesus is the *name* of God, and He desires to live in each of us. This truth has been well communicated in previous chapters, but in Revelation 3:20, Jesus makes it plain: "Behold, I'm standing at the door, knocking. If your heart is open to hear my voice and you open the door within, I will come in to you." And John wrote further on in Revelation 21:3, "I heard a thunderous voice from the throne, saying: 'Look! God's tabernacle is with human beings. And from now on he will tabernacle with them as their God. Now God himself will have his home with them—"God-with-them" will be their God!'"

In the Greek, the word "tabernacle" in the verse above means a tent or cloth hut, much like the movable temple of God. It is close in meaning to vessel or shadow, which points to the truth that we are vessels of God that are designed to live under His Shadow. Where it says, "God himself will have his *home* with them," other translations read, "he will *dwell* with them" (emphasis added). Both hold the meaning "to occupy" or "reside." God wants to tabernacle with us. He is a tent for us, but we are also a tent for Him. The plan was always for us to dwell in Him and for Him to live at home in us.

In order for God to tabernacle with us, we must *embrace and take hold of His name.* We must grab hold of Him with a passionate embrace of love that draws us into deeper intimacy with Him, which in turn empowers us to live according to His Word. Jesus Himself told us, "Loving me empowers you to obey my word. And my Father will love you so deeply that we will come to you and make you our dwelling place" (John 14:23). Obeying His Word is a response of love, and our obedience creates space for a greater measure of His love to occupy our hearts.

A Closer Look at Embrace

In chapter one, I shared my basic understanding of embrace to indicate intimacy and determined intention. It means clasping in one's arms with the sentiment of cherishing and love. To embrace is to gladly take up something and can mean to take in or include it as a part of a more inclusive whole. Even more, it can mean to be equal or equivalent to another.[2]

Let's take a moment to meditate on these meanings. Imagine yourself clasping Jesus in your arms. Cherishing Him. Loving everything about Him. Holding Him as the authority of your life. Envision yourself gladly taking Him up, or as John 1:12 says, "taking hold" of His very essence. Think of the names that have resonated the deepest within you as you have read this book. Can you see yourself embracing those characteristics with no hesitation and being shaped and molded by them?

Now...here's a big one. The last meaning listed is to be equal or equivalent to. According to 1 John 4:17, "all that Jesus now is, so are we in this world," and when speaking to His bride in the Song of Songs, Jesus calls her, "My equal" (4:9–10; 5:1). By the work of the cross, His shed blood, and His resurrection, we have been made equal to Jesus because we are one with Him. Embracing the name of Jesus means that we take hold of who we are *in Him*, who He has made us to be—holy, righteous, and a reflection of His glory—right now, while we still live on earth.

Paul said it well in Ephesians 4:24, "Be transformed as you *embrace the glorious Christ-within as your new life and live in union with him! For God has re-created you all over again in his perfect righteousness, and you now belong to him in the realm of true holiness*" (emphasis added). To live in union with Jesus is to live in a divine embrace with His nature.

Have you ever participated in a group hug? If so, you know that only one person can occupy the space directly in front of your heart. To truly embrace Jesus in a manner He is worthy of, we must cherish Him above all, keeping Him front and center in our lives, absorbing Him into our very being. All other loves and passions are then filtered through Him.

A Practical Embrace

I hope by now you agree that the name of Jesus is so much more than J-e-s-u-s. I also hope that I've clearly communicated that *embracing and taking hold of* Jesus' name is more than making a statement of faith, but rather including Him in who we are as a whole being. Life in Christ is not possible without being...well...*in* Him. We can follow rules and talk about Him. We can read the Bible, go to church, and do good things, but without *know*ing Him, it is all for nothing in the scope of eternity. However, by living *in* Him and Him living *in* us, He gives us the authority to be children of God and helps our yielded hearts discover more of Him each day.

By taking hold of Jesus and all He is, we spend our lives getting to *know* Him by living in His presence. As we do, we grow in our ability to reveal Him to others by manifesting His character as our own. Jesus explained in John 14:6–7, "I am the Way, I am the Truth, and I am the Life. No one comes next to the Father except through union with me. To *know* me is to *know* my Father too. And from now on you will realize that you have seen him and *experienced* him" (emphasis added). Remember that one of the meanings of *know* is to have *experience of.*

Embracing Jesus' name, His character, His authority, the essence of who He is, and all the different aspects we have covered and all those we haven't, requires the laying down of other names, false gods, and the worship of them. Embracing His Name requires seeking Him above all others, and obeying His Word, not from obligation or expectation, but from an intimate, loving relationship with Him. "Jesus said to those Jews who believed in him, 'When you continue to embrace all that I teach, you prove that you are my true followers. For if you embrace the truth, it will release true freedom into your lives'" (John 8:31–32).

God desires an embrace with us that is practical. He wants us to actively live from our embrace with Him, applying our knowledge of who He is in our everyday experiences. This is what His true followers do. To live with a form of godliness or a display of pretense but refuse to live in a practical relationship with Him is empty religion. The religious leaders of Jesus' day provide a clear example of this.

Their response to Jesus was the same as the Israelites' response to Jeremiah when he called them to the crossroads. When he told them to consider their ways, he was telling them to evaluate themselves—to thoughtfully consider the motivation behind their actions. They had been seduced by the cultures around them, so when Jeremiah told them to ask for the ancient path, they said, "We will not. That's not the path we want" (Jeremiah 6:16).

Barriers to Embrace

How similar it is to the modern-day church. While people may not say those words, their actions do. So many who proclaim faith in Jesus have been seduced into tolerating what opposes Him. Simultaneously, many have aligned with the cravings of the self-life, such as what Paul listed in Galatians 5:19–21:

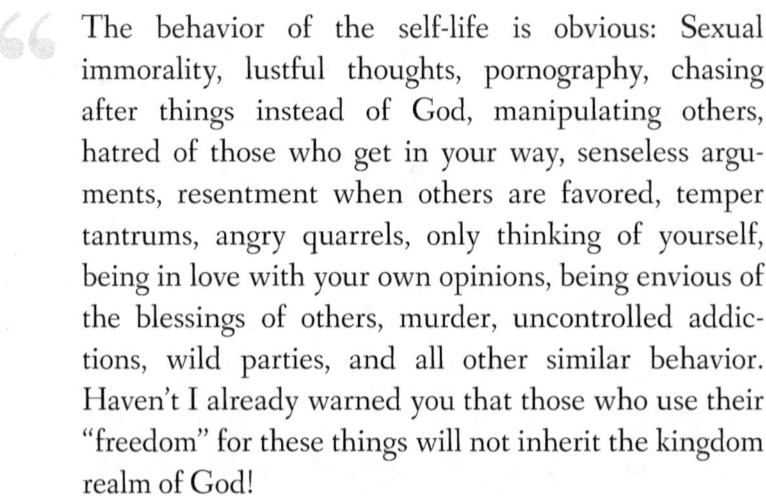

> The behavior of the self-life is obvious: Sexual immorality, lustful thoughts, pornography, chasing after things instead of God, manipulating others, hatred of those who get in your way, senseless arguments, resentment when others are favored, temper tantrums, angry quarrels, only thinking of yourself, being in love with your own opinions, being envious of the blessings of others, murder, uncontrolled addictions, wild parties, and all other similar behavior. Haven't I already warned you that those who use their "freedom" for these things will not inherit the kingdom realm of God!

Remember my struggle that I shared in chapter one? I was so desperate for Jesus to move in some situations in my life, but He wasn't answering my prayers or seeming to respond when I spoke His name. Part of the process He took me through, after prompting me to learn the meaning of *name*, was identifying areas of my life that were entrenched in the self-life. My internal pain from past hurts manifested regularly in ugly behaviors that, unknown to me, were subconscious attempts to protect me from more hurt. This self-life pattern kept me from experiencing the answers, healing, and deliverance I needed and ultimately from *knowing* Jesus at a deeper level of intimacy.

The challenges in my life were valid. While many came from a build-up of subconscious emotional distress, some were brought on by situations outside of myself. Regardless of the origin, I needed help getting out of the pit of despair I was in. Can you relate? Thankfully, God doesn't leave us in our struggle! He never highlights our shortcomings or sin just for the sake of pointing them out or to bring shame. His purpose is to reveal what He wants to free us from so that we have space to receive what He desires to fill us with.

Paul, by the unction of Holy Spirit, identified the self-life to bring awareness of what is hindering us from experiencing the Kingdom of God in our lives, the portion of our inheritance to be manifested here on earth. Any behavior or habit that we allow to occupy space in our hearts or lives that doesn't align with the character and authority of Jesus is an idol and possibly a god that we serve, whether listed in the passage above or not. Whatever it is, it has to go if we want to embrace the fullness of who Jesus is.

In alignment with the nature of God, Paul didn't stop after identifying self-life characteristics, he also taught how to overcome them: "As you yield to the dynamic life and power of the Holy Spirit, you will abandon the cravings of your self-life" (Galatians 5:16). He demonstrated the heart of God by calling the Body of Christ higher, to live by the Spirit of God instead of the flesh.

Benefits of the Embrace

Paul went on to reveal what is available to all believers who yield to the Spirit of God as a way of life:

> But the fruit produced by the Holy Spirit within you is divine love in all its varied expressions: joy that overflows, peace that subdues, patience that endures, kindness in action, a life full of virtue, faith that prevails, gentleness of heart, and strength of spirit. Never set the law above these qualities, for they are meant to be limitless. ... If the Spirit is the source of our life, we must also allow the Spirit to direct every aspect of our lives.
>
> — Galatians 5:22–23, 25

This sounds a lot like *embracing and taking hold of* the life Jesus came to give us, doesn't it? Just as Adam was embraced by the hand of Yahweh as He fashioned him, each of us was embraced by Jesus. He took up our sin in His flesh and became equal to us as He hung on the cross, taking our punishment so we could be free. He embraced all of humanity in the hope that all humans would reciprocate, that we would *embrace and take hold of His name.*

Just as He spoke through Jeremiah, saying, "Consider your ways and ask for the ancient paths. Walk on his [God's] path" and just as He spoke through John the Baptist, "Keep turning away from evil and turn back to God," He speaks to us now by His Spirit. His still, small voice is beckoning His people to destroy the altars that elevate false gods and idols in our lives. He is calling out, seeking a place for His name to dwell, for His character and nature to be displayed in a pure vessel. But He won't dwell in mixture. He can't. And we cannot offer worship to Jesus with a divided heart.

We are at a pivotal time in the earth. It is time to open our hearts to Jesus and embrace His name in purity. How can we be certain, though, that we are following Jesus rightly? By seeking Him with a pure heart and asking Him to reveal anything that may be hindering deeper intimacy and the ability to hear Him with clarity. And when

He does, we must repent, laying it all down for Jesus. Then take hold of what He has provided to fill that void.

Embracing Jesus means we embrace holiness because He is holy. Since He is righteousness, we embrace righteousness—we take His righteousness into ourselves. Jesus revealed the nature of God as a humble servant, so we embrace humility and live accordingly. Scripture reveals His character, and as we read His Word with hearts seeking to know Him more, Holy Spirit highlights which attribute He wants to further develop in us as we *embrace His name.*

As we spend time in God's presence, in the secret place, seeking His face, we get to know Him more intimately. We learn His voice more clearly. We are drawn into alignment with Him and begin to manifest His character. Our understanding becomes more enlightened in the situations we face daily. There truly is power in the name of Jesus, and as we enter a practical embrace with the essence of who Jesus is, the things of this world and the desires of the flesh nature begin to fade away.

My greatest desire for you after exploring these different names of Jesus is that you would choose to embrace Him more fully and continue to explore all of who Jesus is for you. He is unquestionably the Son of the living God. He is undeniably the Savior of the world and is unequivocally the Lord that all will bow before. Consider regularly revisiting Jesus' question, "Who do you say I am?" Or maybe turn it around and ask Him, "Jesus, who (or what) do You want to be for me today (or in this situation)?"

I hope by now you have joined me in the realization that the answer is ever-expanding as we grow in *knowing* Him. As the "I AM that I AM," He is everything that we need and so much more. I also hope that as you grow in knowing Him, your comprehension of the depth of His never-ending, unconditional love grows as well. God Almighty knows you, loves you, and longs for your embrace.

Who Is Jesus to You?

As we position ourselves in Him by faith, surrender to His authority, and align with His character, we make room for Jesus to dwell. As children of God, we will experience Him in growing measures and will continue cultivating deeper intimacy with Him by *embracing and taking hold of His name.*

Points to Ponder

- In what way have you heard Him beckon you to the ancient path?
- What aspects of the self-life did the Holy Spirit bring to your attention? Spend some time offering your heart to Him as you lay down whatever it is that may hold a higher position in your heart than Jesus. Invite Him to come and cleanse and renew your heart to be fully devoted to Him.
- List at least one way Jesus is currently inviting you to embrace His Name.
- Who is Jesus to you?

Prayer of Embrace

Thank You, Jesus, for everything You are and everything You have done for me. Thank You for embracing me as You hung on the cross so that I can embrace You. I surrender my life to You afresh today. I choose to seek to know You more intimately and to live from the place of dwelling in You. I commit to embracing every aspect of who You are as You continue to reveal Yourself to me and envelop me in Your essence. Thank You for giving me the authority to be Your child. I love you, Jesus, and I embrace Your name. Amen.

Notes

1. What Is in a Name?

1. Doug Hershey, "Yeshua: The Meaning of the Hebrew Name of Jesus," FIRM Israel, December 22, 2015, https://firmisrael.org/learn/who-is-yeshua-meaning-of-hebrew-name-jesus/.
2. Merriam-Webster.com Dictionary, s.v. "know," accessed June 2, 2022, https://www.merriam-webster.com/dictionary/know.
3. Merriam-Webster.com Dictionary, s.v. "absolutely," accessed June 2, 2022, https://www.merriam-webster.com/dictionary/absolutely
4. Strong's Greek: 3686. ὄνομα (onoma) -- a name, authority, cause. (n.d.). Retrieved October 18, 2022, from https://biblehub.com/greek/3686.htm
5. Merriam-Webster.com Dictionary, s.v. "manifestation," accessed May 31, 2022, https://www.merriam-webster.com/dictionary/manifestation
6. Merriam-Webster.com Dictionary, s.v. "revelation," accessed May 31, 2022, https://www.merriam-webster.com/dictionary/revelation
7. Merriam-Webster.com Dictionary, s.v. "distinguish," accessed May 31, 2022, https://www.merriam-webster.com/dictionary/distinguish
8. Merriam-Webster.com Dictionary, s.v. "essence," accessed June 1, 2022, https://www.merriam-webster.com/dictionary/essence.

2. Who Do You Say I Am?

1. See Matthew 12:25 and Luke 6:8.
2. See 1 Corinthians 6:17.
3. See John 1:1, 10:30.
4. From TPT footnotes on Genesis 1:1.
5. From TPT footnotes on Genesis 2:4.
6. From TPT footnotes on Genesis 14:19.
7. From TPT footnotes on Psalm 91:1.
8. From TPT footnotes on Genesis 22:14.
9. See Genesis 22:1–14.

3. The Building Blocks of Knowing Jesus

1. See Matthew 7:21–23.
2. See Hebrews 12:2.
3. Merriam-Webster.com Dictionary, s.v. "authority," accessed February 10, 2025, https://www.merriam-webster.com/dictionary/authority.

4. See 1 Samuel 16:7 and 1 Kings 8:39.
5. See Matthew 6:33.

4. Master Designer and Creator

1. See John 4:16.

5. Redeemer

1. Merriam-Webster.com Dictionary, s.v. "deem," accessed September 25, 2024, https://www.merriam-webster.com/dictionary/deem
2. See Esther 4.
3. See Esther 5–7.
4. See Esther 8:5, 7–8.
5. See Genesis 1:27–28.
6. See Revelation 13:8.
7. Merriam-Webster.com Dictionary, s.v. "redeem," accessed September 13, 2024, https://www.merriam-webster.com/dictionary/redeem
8. Merriam-Webster.com Dictionary, s.v. "redeem," accessed September 13, 2024, https://www.merriam-webster.com/dictionary/redeem
9. See John 10:10.
10. See Ephesians 2:2.
11. See John 10:10.
12. See Matthew 4:4, 7, and 10.
13. See Isaiah 55:10–11.
14. See John 1:1–5.
15. See Ephesians 6:11–12.

6. A Friend Like No Other

1. Merriam-Webster.com Dictionary, s.v. "friend," accessed January 20, 2023, https://www.merriam-webster.com/dictionary/friend
2. ChaimBentorah, "Hebrew (Aramaic Word Study – Bond Servants," Chaim Bentorah, October 4, 2019, https://tinyurl.com/2chbzx69.
3. ChaimBentorah, "Hebrew (Aramaic Word Study – Bond Servants," Chaim Bentorah, October 4, 2019, https://tinyurl.com/2chbzx69.Bentorah, Bond Servants.

7. The Good Shepherd

1. See TPT footnote on Psalm 23:1.
2. Merriam-Webster.com Dictionary, s.v. "scion," accessed November 13, 2024, https://www.merriam-webster.com/dictionary/scion.
3. See Isaiah 11:1.

4. Jeff A. Benner, "Manners & Customs: Shepherd Life; the Care of Sheep and Goats: AHRC," Manners & Customs: Shepherd life; the care of sheep and goats | AHRC, accessed November 13, 2024, https://www.ancient-hebrew.org/manners/shepherd-life-the-care-of-sheep-and-goats.htm.

5. Nancy Stoppe, "Inspirational Insights: The Voice of the Shepherd," Daily American, April 11, 2022, https://www.dailyamerican.com/story/opinion/columns/2022/04/11/nancy-stoppe-column-about-the-voice-of-the-shepherd/65348836007/#.

8. Comforting Staff

1. See Psalm 40:2.

9. Curator

1. Merriam-Webster.com Dictionary, s.v. "curate," accessed November 13, 2024, https://www.merriam-webster.com/dictionary/curate.

2. Oxford English Dictionary, s.v. "curate (n.), sense I.1.a," March 2024, https://doi.org/10.1093/OED/8420559653.

3. From TPT footnotes on Mathew 2:23.

4. See John 14:12.

5. See Ephesians 1:9.

10. Revelation-Light, More Than Just a Light

1. Merriam-Webster.com Dictionary, s.v. "revelation," accessed June 2, 2024, https://www.merriam-webster.com/dictionary/revelation

2. See Isaiah 9:2; 40:5; 42:6; 49:6; 51:4; 60:1–3.

3. From TPT footnotes on Matthew 4:16.

4. See John 3:16–18.

5. See John 8:12.

11. Rebel, Revolutionary, or Both?

1. See Matthew 12:38–39, and 16:1–4.

2. Anne Douglas Sedgwick. AZQuotes.com, Wind and Fly LTD, 2025. https://www.azquotes.com/quote/1194602, accessed February 12, 2025.

3. Merriam-Webster.com Dictionary, s.v. "rebellion," accessed June 19, 2024, https://www.merriam-webster.com/dictionary/rebellion.

4. Merriam-Webster.com Dictionary, s.v. "revolution," accessed June 19, 2024, https://www.merriam-webster.com/dictionary/revolution.

5. Aristotle. AZQuotes.com, Wind and Fly LTD, 2025. https://www.azquotes.com/quote/10340, accessed February 12, 2025.

12. Resurrection

1. Merriam-Webster.com Dictionary, s.v. "resurrection," accessed June 19, 2024, https://www.merriam-webster.com/dictionary/resurrection
2. See 2 Corinthians 3:18.
3. See Hebrews 12:2.
4. See Romans 8:11.
5. See Ephesians 2:6.

13. Breath of Heaven

1. See John 20:21–23.

15. Ultimate Example

1. See John 21:25.

16. Rest

1. See John 14:6.
2. See Mark 4:37–38.

17. King Eternal

1. Merriam-Webster.com Dictionary, s.v. "king," accessed February 12, 2024, https://www.merriam-webster.com/dictionary/king
2. *The Lion King*, DVD (United States, United States: Buena Vista Pictures, Walt Disney Home Video : Distributed by Buena Vista Home Video, 1994).
3. See Hebrews 1:8.
4. See John 3:3, 5, 11; 5:19, 24, 25; 8:34, 51, 58.
5. See 2 Corinthians 3:18.
6. See Hebrews 7:1.
7. See Hebrews 7:23.
8. See Hebrews 7:25.

18. Twofold Fire

1. See Daniel 3.
2. See Leviticus 9:24.
3. Merriam-Webster.com Dictionary, s.v. "baptism of fire," accessed April 10, 2023, https://www.merriam-webster.com/dictionary/baptism%20of%20fire.
4. See Romans 8:26–27 and Jude 20.

5. Merriam-Webster.com Dictionary, s.v. "baptism of fire," accessed April 10, 2023, https://www.merriam-webster.com/dictionary/baptism%20of%20fire.
6. See 1 Peter 3:21.
7. See Mark 9:50.

19. Heavenly Captor

1. Merriam-Webster.com Dictionary, s.v. "captive," accessed September 25, 2023, https://www.merriam-webster.com/dictionary/captive.)
2. Merriam-Webster.com Dictionary, s.v. "captor," accessed October 3, 2023, https://www.merriam-webster.com/dictionary/captor.
3. See Psalm 23:2.
4. See Ephesians 2:6.
5. See Ephesians 4:1.
6. See Song of Songs 1:6 and 5:7.
7. See Luke 17:21.

20. Unshakable Foundation

1. Adriana Tomiša, "A Case of Foundation Soil Failure - the Transcona Grain Elevator," Geotech, February 22, 2023, https://www.geotech.hr/en/case-of-foun dation-soil-failure-transcona-grain-elevator/.
2. See Romans 3:23.
3. From TPT footnotes on Ephesians 1:4.
4. Robby Galatty, "The Forgotten Jesus Part 2: Was Jesus a Carpenter or a Stonemason?," Lifeway Leadership, September 26, 2018, https://leadership.lifeway.com/2017/04/04/the-forgotten-jesus-part-2-was-jesus-a-carpenter-or-a-stonema son/.
5. Taken from the TPT footnotes on this verse.

21. Embrace His Name

1. See Deuteronomy 12:1–5.
2. Merriam-Webster.com Dictionary, s.v. "embrace," accessed October 23, 2024, https://www.merriam-webster.com/dictionary/embrace.

Acknowledgments

This book exists by the grace of God. The message of *Who Is Jesus to You* was birthed in my heart during a lengthy time of personal struggle. During that time, I repeatedly heard Jesus ask me, "Who am I to you?"

This question burned in my heart, provoking me to pursue Him more intimately and helping me to see Him in the practical details of everyday life. Jesus began revealing Himself to me in light of His characteristics and expanding my understanding of His name.

After carrying and developing the message in my heart for several years, I needed help getting the book written, and the Lord connected me with Messenger Books. Thank you, Jeremiah and Teresa Yancy, for teaching me step by step and walking with me through the process of writing this book. Thank you for speaking life into my once weary soul, encouraging me, and reminding me regularly that I have been given a message that needs to be shared. You both championed me when I desperately needed it and brought out the gold that had been buried for a long time. I am eternally grateful for your leadership and your friendship.

I want to acknowledge the entire Messenger Books Team, those who are behind the scenes with the technical and digital aspects of writing and publishing, creating, and marketing. Also, those Messengers who are already successful authors and have partnered with the

Messenger Life community to teach, encourage, build up, and speak life to those of us just beginning.

Thank you to my friends and family who have encouraged me and prayed for me throughout the writing of this book. I am grateful.

About the Author

Jeni LaGore is passionate about knowing Jesus in an extraordinary way. She has served in the local church as a youth pastor, minister's assistant, and in women's and children's ministries, as well as in many behind-the-scenes duties for the household of God. However, Jeni considers her marriage and her children her greatest achievement and the greatest ministry she has ever had. The Lord has recently called her to found "At Home Ministries," where she encourages the Body of Christ to live At Home in Jesus and to welcome Him to live At Home in them. Jeni lives in Michigan with her husband, Shane.